LIFETIMES

*Spiritual Explorations of Earth and
Galactic Past Lives*

Enjoy these other books in the Common Sentience series:

AKASHA: *Spiritual Experiences of Accessing the Infinite Intelligence of Our Souls*
by Lisa Barnett

ANCESTORS: *Divine Remembrances of Lineage, Relations and Sacred Sites*
by Mindahi Bastida

ANGELS: *Personal Encounters with Divine Beings of Light*
by Tricia McCannon

ANIMALS: *Personal Tales of Encounters with Spirit Animals*
by Dr. Steven Farmer

ASCENSION: *Divine Stories of Awakening the Whole and Holy Being Within*
by William Henry

GODDESS: *Blessed Reunions with the Feminine Face of the Divine*
by Anodea Judith

GODTALK: *Experiences of Humanity's Connections with a Higher Power*
by Neale Donald Walsch

GUIDES: *Mystical Connections to Soul Guides and Divine Teachers*
by Marilyn Alauria

MEDITATION: *Intimate Experiences with the Divine through Contemplative Practices*
by Sister Dr. Jenna

MEDIUMSHIP: *Sacred Communications with Loved Ones from Across the Veil*
by Suzanne Giesemann

NATURE: *Divine Experiences with Trees, Plants, Stones and Landscapes*
by Ana Maria Vasquez

PORTALS: *Energetic Doorways to Mystical Experiences Between Worlds*
by Freddy Silva

SHAMANISM: *Personal Quests of Communion with Nature and Creation*
by Oscar Miro-Quesada

SIGNS: *Sacred Encounters with Pathways, Turning Points, and Divine Guideposts*
by Simran

SOUND: *Profound Experiences with Chanting, Toning, Music and Healing Frequencies*
by Drs. JJ and Desiree Hurtak

WITCH: *Divine Alignments with the Primordial Energies of
Magick and Cycles of Nature*
by Valerie Love

Learn more at sacredstories.com

LIFETIMES

Spiritual Explorations of Earth and Galactic Past Lives

ADAM APOLLO

Sacred Stories
PUBLISHING

Lifetimes
Spiritual Explorations of Earth and Galactic Past Lives

Adam Apollo

Print ISBN: 978-1-958921-76-0
Ebook ISBN: 978-1-958921-77-7
Library of Congress Control Number: 2025944584

Published by Sacred Stories Publishing, Fort Lauderdale, FL USA

CONTENTS

PART THREE: EXPERIENCING YOUR PAST LIVES

PART ONE

Understanding Past Lives

You were born with wings, why prefer to crawl through life?

— RUMI

THE SOUL'S JOURNEY

When we consider who we are, we often reflect on the events of our lives. We know that each experience, each relationship, and each identity we choose comes to define us. The actions we take generate feedback that helps us grow, evolve, and discover more of what is possible.

We may identify with our failures, or we may identify with our successes. The choice is ultimately ours at every moment. More importantly, we face a critical juncture at some point in our journey of self-development: If we truly reflect on our lives, accepting all that has happened and everything it has led to, is it truly possible to fail at all? Or is every event just part of a greater journey, a path of self-discovery, of pain and healing, of broken relationships and exquisite soul reunions full of love?

When we discover this greater journey and begin to understand the events of our lives as part of a grand tapestry woven through the wisdom of our souls, we find that everything that has happened to us has happened *for us*. The steps of self-realization we have taken reach far back in time, and the braids of our connections with other people, places, ideas, wisdom, skills, and inherent gifts stretch across many more lifetimes than one.

Every spiritual tradition on Earth describes the soul in one way or another, which generally involves connecting with that aspect of ourselves that is more than just the physical body. Many conscious practices across different cultures help us access this biofield of energy, revealing that we are more than just thick matter. Whether discussed as the foundation to health and skillful movement, like *chi* or *prana,* or articulated as the fundamental field of all creation, with terms like *Great Spirit, Odic field,* or even the *Higgs field,* we are currently witnessing the emergence of new science alongside the resurfacing of ancient wisdom.

Leading-edge unified physics provides frameworks and solutions for understanding spiritual aspects of reality directly in conjunction with the material aspects of reality, revealing that *spacetime*—a mathematical model that combines the three physical dimensions and the fourth dimension of time into a single, four-dimensional continuum—itself has functions of memory, information exchange, and intelligent feedback mechanisms.

Through this lens, we begin to understand that quantum mechanics is simply describing an energetic structure, a highly coherent field that we, as souls, inhabit.

It is not that consciousness arises exclusively through the incarnation of a soul, but that it is an integral part of the entire universe at every level. However, each soul is a completely individuated essence, a *prime number*, differentiated and evolving, the fruit of consciousness.

You are infinitely individual. Only you have had your collection of experiences, relationships, thoughts, feelings, and physical sensations.

Yet here's the big question: When did you *start* experiencing?

Notice that only you know when you started experiencing things based on your memory. You might remember being very young in childhood, but before that, things are a bit murkier.

However, if you carefully consider your life, you'll also find that there have been many things that came naturally to you, as well as gifts and interests that didn't match those of your parents or ancestors. Some of us feel completely different from our families, as though we are some strange visitors from another family entirely. This is not far from the truth.

Why do we feel deeply interested and inspired by certain periods in history but not others? I would often feel like I wanted to fall asleep in history class, but then, for certain eras, I would light up like fireworks. I couldn't stop looking at the pictures, reading about the events, and exploring the weapons and tools of the culture and period.

Consider that, as a soul, you may have chosen to incarnate in many bodies across many time periods. Incarnating is essentially migrating from a spiritual plane of existence to one where your soul uses a physical body, forming in a womb that matches your soul's desire for experience and growth.

Many cultures around the world consider reincarnation the act of incarnating many times in different bodies, as a foundation of their entire way of life and understanding. People practicing Hinduism have various perspectives on reincarnation. Some are extremely limiting, such as the caste system based on karma, while others are highly empowering, like the art of tantra and kundalini yoga, both soul-liberating practices.

Some traditions hold the perspective that all is illusion, and the ultimate goal is to free the self from any sense of individuality. Yet other traditions suggest that we are already infinite, and the experience of our individuality is the ultimate path to divinity.

Taking the Taoist view of yin and yang and applying it to these various belief systems, we can see that this is all a dance of consciousness. When we journey on the path of liberation, we find ourselves becoming more deeply present in who we are as individuals. As we anchor and ground in our individuality and open to all experiences, desires, and life events, we expand into a deeper understanding of the collective, the whole.

Whether we believe either path is good or bad determines our perception and experience; each path leads to the same self-realization.

What if you could remember skills you developed across your past lifetimes? If you've incarnated many times (five, ten, one hundred?), what kind of library of experiences and abilities have you cultivated? What if you could recall languages you spoke in the past, or cultures you were a part of, making it easier to embody them now? What if you could remember people you knew in other lifetimes, instantly rekindling the connection, trust, love, and growth you went through together? What if you have already had these types of experiences, but you have not been aware of what is happening?

Those moments of *déjà vu*, waves of deep familiarity upon meeting someone, that love at first sight magic... these experiences are often intersections in time, where the past and present converge through the resonance of the moment.

These moments seem to defy explanation, but within them lie the secrets to discovering *who we are*. We might stand in an ancient place for the first time and our chest tightens with a grief we can't name ... or we meet someone and feel as though we have loved them for a thousand years in an instant. Or a language we've never studied rolls off our tongue in our dreams.

These are not fantasies. They are *whispers from the soul*.

Past life recall does not always occur through grand visions or dramatic regressions. Sometimes it can be more subtle, in the tickles of a remembered dream, emotions from a scent, or even strange sensations suddenly arising in the body. Sometimes memories from other lives can surface as an irrational fear or an unexplainable aversion. Sometimes, it may even bloom into reawakened gifts: skills we never studied, instruments we never learned, or talents that come naturally, as easily as breathing.

While the pain and fear that might arise near deep, dark water may be unsettling to face, gaining awareness that you drowned in a past life can help you not only clear that phobia, but also unlock knowledge and skills from that life. If you spent lifetimes as a warrior using weapons to defend, fight, and kill, then practicing with those same weapons for personal strength and focus in this life can also help you heal and transmute the pain of those past life battles.

Just as facing the wounds of childhood helps us grow beyond old patterns and somatic pain, embracing our past lifetimes can accelerate our healing and soul evolution.

It is not important whether we come to *believe* in reincarnation. What matters is whether we are willing to be curious about who we really are. When we open that doorway, we begin to integrate parts of ourselves we didn't even know were missing.

This is the true power of past life remembrance: It can heal our sense of fragmentation and our feelings of displacement or loss of belonging.

It returns our soul to *wholeness.*

As we remember, we begin to walk differently in this life. We stop fearing death because we know we have lived before. We have greater compassion for others because we know what it is like to have gone through something similar. Perhaps we've experienced being a victim, a perpetrator, or a hero, and we've discovered the pain and *karma* incurred in each of these roles. We stop clinging to control because we've seen the great weave of lifetimes, and we remember the perfection in its patterns. We approach relationships with more reverence because we know that love is never lost, only transformed through time.

You may not remember yet. But your soul remembers.

It is patient. It is wise. And it is waiting.

EVIDENCE OF PAST LIFE RECALL

O ver the last century, researchers around the world have investigated people, especially children—who recall vivid, accurate details of lifetimes they could not have learned about through ordinary means. These memories sometimes include names, languages, customs, geographic descriptions, and even deaths that later prove verifiable through historical records. As more data has emerged, the validity of this field of inquiry has become difficult to dismiss.

One of the most well-respected pioneers in this work is Dr. Ian Stevenson, former Head of Psychiatry at the University of Virginia. Over more than four decades, Stevenson examined over 2,500 cases of children from around the world who spontaneously recalled previous lives. His research was meticulous and deeply documented.

In many instances, he traced their memories to real individuals who had lived and died, finding surprising matches between the child's statements and the details of the deceased's life including not only names and events, but specific injuries, habits, and even birthmarks that corresponded to the cause of death.

In one case, a child recalled his prior name, family, and how he was killed in a village conflict; researchers later confirmed the story—and the physical birthmark on the child's body aligned with the fatal wound of the man he claimed to have been. This data strongly implies that there is a direct physiological connection between lives.

GENETIC ROOTS

Since my work in 2004 with BioVision 2020, where I contributed to extensive research and talks on epigenetics and the problems with genetic modification in its current state, I have theorized that there is a connection between lifetimes that is genetic in nature.

When we look at DNA, we see two clear genetic roots in each of the blood parents of that individual, and yet there is a tremendous amount of DNA which has an unknown pattern and origin. Dr. Sonia Contera, Professor of Biological Physics at the University of Oxford is known to have said, "98 percent of DNA is a mystery."

What if there is a hidden code, woven into our DNA, carrying information across lifetimes into each of our bodies?

CHILDREN WITH MEMORY

Dr. Jim Tucker, Stevenson's successor at UVA's Division of Perceptual Studies, has continued and expanded work on past life cases where there is extremely detailed knowledge and recollection, as well as physiological impacts from the memories.

Among his best-known investigations is the case of James Leininger, a boy from Louisiana who, between the ages of two and five, vividly described being a World War II fighter pilot. He named the aircraft carrier *Natoma Bay* and recalled specific technical details about the planes and described being shot down near Iwo Jima. All of these details, including the pilot's name and military records, were later confirmed by researchers. Even his airplane was found hidden under the ocean in the area he remembered crashing. James also recognized other pilots from photographs and exhibited behaviors, dreams, and knowledge far beyond what could be explained by coincidence or imagination.

What makes these cases so compelling is that they often arise in very young children, sometimes as early as two or three years old—and do so spontaneously, without prompting. The memories tend to fade as the child ages, especially once they feel a sense of resolution or closure around the past life. These factors help distinguish genuine past life memory from confabulation or fantasy. In many instances, the children exhibit emotional intensity or unusual behaviors related to the life they describe. They may display fears or affinities that mirror their past experiences, such as avoiding water if they drowned, or gravitating toward specific regions or vocations related to their previous identity.

REGRESSION & HYPNOSIS

Adults also report memories of other lives, although these often surface through regression techniques—guided hypnosis, deep meditation, trauma healing, or even dream states.

Dr. Helen Wambach, a clinical psychologist and researcher, regressed more than 1,000 subjects in the 1970s and '80s to explore this phenomenon. Her subjects described scenes from a vast range of time periods and civilizations. What stood out, however, was the consistency of detail. The foods they ate, the clothing styles, currencies used, and roles in society all aligned with what historians later confirmed about those eras, suggesting these were not simply fabricated memories, but something more.

Dr. Brian Weiss, a psychiatrist trained at Yale, was also pulled into this work unexpectedly when a patient under hypnosis began describing lifetimes with remarkable clarity. Her regressions led to emotional breakthroughs and physical healings that conventional therapy had failed to access. Weiss's experience with this and subsequent patients catalyzed his own transformation and inspired his bestselling work, *Many Lives, Many Masters*, which brought the concept of therapeutic past life recall into the mainstream.

NEUROSCIENCE

How can such memories exist if we believe consciousness is generated solely by the brain? Here, modern neuroscience offers an unexpected window. There are increasing signs that the brain may not be the source of consciousness, but rather a receiver—an interface or antenna tuned to access a deeper field of non-local memory. Cases of savants, near-death experiencers, and people with brain damage retaining full memories all suggest that memory does not reside exclusively within the neural pathways of the skull.

Researchers of quantum biology say some brain structures, especially structures known as *microtubules* within neurons are possible conduits of this kind of information. These microscopic channels may allow the brain to access information stored in quantum fields—fields that carry not just present experience, but the residues of every experience the soul has ever had.

YongDeok Cho and his team showed that DNA has a natural capability to control *quantum emitters*, which they describe as "grabbing" and "steering" at the quantum-mechanical level. Their research was fully peer-reviewed in the *Nanophotonics* journal.

What if the metaphysical behaviors of people subconsciously acting out ancestral patterns are due to DNA influencing the microtubule quantum emitters in the brain? And what if that past life information contained in DNA could similarly be accessed in this way?

This model supports the idea that we are not remembering the past so much as tuning into it, like logging into a living database that our own resonance reactivates.

EMOTIONAL IMPRINTS

Even without hypnosis or science, many people experience what I call *soul echoes,* emotional or energetic imprints that surface unexpectedly. A person may feel an overwhelming connection to a culture they have never studied, or a grief so old it defies explanation. Some walk through ancient cities and feel a strange familiarity. Others dream in languages they have never learned. These are the glimmers—small but powerful fragments of memory trying to reach the surface.

And how do we know what's real? The most trustworthy past life impressions often carry a specific tone: they are emotionally rich, specific in detail, and resistant to being reshaped by the imagination. They arise unbidden, sometimes in dreams, sometimes in relationships, sometimes in unexpected emotional reactions to music, landscapes, or even objects. When we experience a soul-trigger, something deep inside stirs—not just with curiosity, but with a sense of *recognition.*

THE LEADING EDGE

Emerging research and experiential reports suggest something astonishing: The soul may operate across lifetimes as a single, continuous consciousness, encoding its experience not only into subtle fields of energy, but into space itself—into the quantum fabric of spacetime. With each life, we do not erase our past. We add to it. We evolve.

While mainstream science is only beginning to entertain the possibilities, the evidence is already mounting. Thousands of cases now exist across multinational studies revealing patterns that defy chance.

PERSONAL RESEARCH

In my personal research, I've worked with many hundreds of people with past life memories. Some of these memories arose through spontaneous recall, where they instantly remembered a place or person, while others arose through dreams and then were confirmed by physical experiences. In addition, many have accessed memories through repeatable hypnosis or past life regression processes.

I've been able to locate some of my lifetimes with high specificity. For example, my memories of being a Samurai in Japan awakened when I was a teenager. I then visited Japan to rediscover details of my actual lifetime there.

As part of my teaching support for spiritual leader Vianna Stibal, founder of Theta Healing, I met two Japanese-English translators. One of them was a historian. I shared many details of my past life memories with her, including a description of my *kamon* or family crest. She knew it was Tokugawa immediately. We then used *kinesiology*, muscle testing, to determine my birth time, which was in late 1605 or early 1606.

Only one male Tokugawa family member was born in that period: *Tokugawa Tadanaga*. I was able to look up my prefecture and areas under my responsibility, and they matched my memories exactly. When I visited the Imperial Gardens of Edo Castle (江戸城, *Edo-jō*) for our photoshoot, my family crest was on the Imperial Armory Storehouse (御武具蔵,*O-Bugu-Gura*) above my head in the shots. The next day when I walked out of the place I was staying, I went directly across the street instead of down the road, and there was a set of Tokugawa armor from the 1600s.

These were only a few of the synchronicities that happened, followed by many more discoveries and deep processes around this past life memory.

Eventually, I listened to *The Book of Five Rings* during a blizzard on the way back to Boulder from Salt Lake City. The first half of the audiobook was a historian's detailed recount of the life of Sensei Miyamoto Musashi, who wrote a treatise on the Mastery of Swordsmanship across five scrolls, each of them representing one of five elements...and not Taoist Five Elements. The elements he chose were Ancient Celtic.

As I listened, my body began to quiver as the historian described how this sword master came to live and train with the Tokugawa family. He had met with Tokugawa general Mizuno Katsunari in 1608, teaching him secret techniques of his sword style. Later, in 1614, he laid siege to Osaka with the Tokugawa Ieyasu, the Shogun of the Tokugawa family, and ten-year-old Tadanaga's older brother. Then by 1633, he began staying with Hosokawa Tadatoshi, *daimyo* of Kumamoto Castle, where the Tokugawa family also trained and lived often. For almost ten years, he was with the Tokugawa, Hosokawa, and other clans, supporting the Shimabara Rebellion and spending time in the Edo province, Tadanaga's eventual prefecture.

The waves of memories poured through me, of years of training with Musashi in my Samurai past life. I was also secretly training a daughter of Hosokawa Tadatoshi, as she was not allowed to train with him, and she became my lover. I was in my twenties, and she was in her late teens. I later rediscovered her as a lover of mine in this life.

By the time the audiobook got to the actual five scrolls, I was having full-blown flashbacks of training with Musashi, and it was as though the words of the scrolls were already etched in my heart forever.

My own past life regression research, and the work of many of the authors and scientists listed in this chapter, only scratches the surface of this area of study. To understand this phenomenon more deeply, we next turn to physics to explore an underlying framework for reality that fully integrates and explains some of the physical aspects of these mysterious events.

THE PHYSICS OF MEMORY

*W*hat if memory is not confined to the brain? What if *who you are* does not begin at birth, nor end at death, but flows in a continuum—stretching through lifetimes like a river through valleys, changing shape, but never losing its essence?

Modern science, once silent or skeptical about such ideas, is beginning to echo the whispers of ancient civilizations and cultures around the world, where reincarnation is seen as a fundamental part of our reality.

We have already discussed some researchers, psychologists, and physicists who have uncovered data and phenomena that point to the idea that profound memory may not be localized. It may be non-linear, non-local, and deeply entangled with the very structure of reality.

In this chapter we explore the compelling theoretical physics that may explain past life recall—where hard data meets soft mystery, and the laboratory meets the soul.

How do we access information from our past and regain that information in our bodies now? How could specific movements, skills, knowledge, emotions, and energies translate through time into a visceral and direct physical experience across lifetimes?

QUANTUM WORMHOLE NETWORKS

Quantum entanglement has become big headlines everywhere, from science magazines to the largest mainstream publications in the world. The Chinese now hold the world record for teleportation with the farthest distance ever reached, transmitting an entangled molecular state from Earth to a satellite, seemingly instantaneously. Entanglement is commonly thought to happen when photons are split and the two parts are routed to different locations, but any action taken on one part instantly affects the other.

Albert Einstein called this "spooky action at a distance," and it's a well-known and proven phenomenon. Yet the theories behind it lack a fundamental framework. No one really understands how or why it seems like much of the universe is already entangled.

John Wheeler, author of the college textbook *Gravitation*, proposed that micro-wormhole networks may be behind this phenomenon. Einstein and Nathan Rosen explored the potential of spacetime to curve far enough so that two distant locations could open a *wormhole* between them, a portal between two points in spacetime.

Wheeler and colleagues proposed that these wormholes could also connect quantum fields, and that these kinds of spacetime portals could form a lattice across the universe. They connected what were two seemingly different ideas: entanglement and wormhole theory. This fusion is known as ER=EPR, honoring Einstein and Rosen for their paper on wormholes or "Einstein-Rosen-bridges," and Boris Podolsky, who collaborated with these two for a paper on entanglement (Einstein-Podolsky-Rosen EPR).

THE PATTERN OF SPACETIME

Other physicists, including Lee Smolin, author of *Three Roads to Quantum Gravity*, proposed a similar idea in their theory of how gravity works at scales smaller than our best microscopes can reach. Their equations show a weave of bundles forming the structure of spacetime itself. This weave *is* the "fabric of spacetime" we've all heard about, but rather than a metaphor, he and his colleagues propose it as a tangible structure.

Their greatest limitation, as I perceived it as a seventeen-year-old diving into these books and studies, was a lack of understanding of how the geometry of spacetime would be structured. Their renderings of the fundamental fabric were chaotic, wild triangulations forming blobs and *quantum foam*, a seemingly random froth of energy with no clear structure or pattern.

Yet through my own revelations and awakenings, accessing the inner library of memories I have been building across lifetimes, I knew that the structure must have a pattern. We see these patterns and geometries everywhere, from flowers to hurricanes, galaxies to shells, stone crystals to snowflakes.

I began to see the patterns too and through the work of Buckminster Fuller, who developed the geodesic dome and other profound architectural and geometric innovations, I realized that spacetime is in a state of *tensegrity* where there is an even push and pull between all of the fundamental nodes of energy that make up the fabric of spacetime. This combination of radiation and attractions forces the whole field into equilibrium, so the massive amount of energy in the quantum field comes into balance.

I won't go into depth on the geometry of spacetime in this book, but some important realizations arose from my applications of this study to a deep and foundational understanding of time, memory, and matter.

THE PROTON UNIVERSAL HARD-DRIVE

Through many years of work, I developed an extension of the *Loop Quantum Gravity* theory, where the geometry of the fabric of spacetime is defined, and the way it curves and spins gives rise to all the fundamental forces and functions.

When I focused on the proton as a small, curved area of spacetime—a miniature black hole, as Nassim Haramein proposed in his paper *The Schwarzschild Proton*—I found some startling correlations between the quantum gravitational structure of the proton and the age of the universe.

Based on Haramein's groundbreaking calculations of the generalized number of *Planck Spherical Units* or *PSU*, the quantum bundles of spacetime or quantum information bits in a proton, he found the volume to be 10^{60}.

As someone who has written college level courses on unified physics, the work of Max Planck and Planck units are fundamental to my research, and so I was curious to find out how many units of Planck time—known as *Planck seconds,* a small fraction of our normal seconds, there have been in the lifetime of the universe.

I was stunned to discover the answer: 8×10^{60}.

This means that over the lifetime of the universe, every eight Planck seconds corresponds to one new quantum bit—or Planck Spherical Unit— inside each proton, matching the same order of magnitude: 10^{60}.

In other words, there is a direct correlation between the number of quantum bits or little energy bundles (PSU) in every proton and the amount of time that the universe has been in existence and growing.

Therefore, in 2019, I first proposed that every proton acts like a hard drive, an information storage system that is growing in direct proportion to the universe.

With each beat of time at the Planck scale, protons pulse with inputs and outputs, rhythmically adding new bits of structure like notes of a Divine symphony. The entire cosmos becomes a living song of entanglement and unfolding memory. And if each proton is an instrument playing a part in this orchestra, then your body is a temple filled with these instruments, resonating with lifetimes of experience, storing the echoes of every love, every loss, every triumph, every vow. You are not just a soul within a body, you are a chorus of selves, singing across time.

Applying Wheeler's entanglement theorem to Haramein's calculations of the number of potential surface connections on each proton, we discover that each proton may be entangled with as many as 10^{40} other protons simultaneously. To put this number in perspective, it is possible that you could connect every star in the entire universe to a single proton in your pinky, as there are only about 10^{22} to 10^{24} estimated stars in the universe. Alternatively, you could connect every single proton in your body ($\sim 10^{28}$) to a different star system and still have 100,000+ protons left to connect to other things.

AKASHIC MEMORY

With these realizations, spacetime starts to look like an advanced, intelligent network, a quantum internet filled with distributed hard drives we call protons. Wherever there is matter, the universe has the capacity to remember everything that has ever happened and instantaneously exchange information across the entire network.

This matches descriptions of the Akashic Records from the ancient Hindu tradition. In their philosophy, there is a concept of *Akasha*, which literally refers to the ether or space itself. In the interpretations of the Theosophical Society and Edgar Cayce, this field is thought to contain the memory of all the activities in existence.

Even the word matter comes from *mater*, which essentially means *mother*. Perhaps the Divine Goddess of ancient traditions is speaking directly to the function of memory in spacetime.

She Who Remembers All.

Imagine the fabric of the universe as a light being woven by the loom of time, each Planck unit connected into threads intersecting in tetrahedral geometries and hexagonal lattices. Protons gather these threads, one by one, to weave growing, spherical bundles of structure and memory. Over the lifetime of the universe, they have gathered billions of years' worth of information—entangled patterns from every interaction, every gaze, every echo of being, stitched into little yarn balls of light and memory we call mass and matter.

Perhaps more personally, it means the rich depth of every moment of our experience is a direct result of the almost unbelievable capacity of our bodies and matter to exchange and store information. Science has often marveled at the capacity for our muscles and tissues to store memory patterns and imprints over years or decades, but the underlying quantum mechanical mechanisms for this have remained a mystery until now.

And so, beneath your skin and behind your eyes, you are not only experiencing the present; you are also carrying the song of the stars, encoded in the silence between beats. You are built of memory, layered in light, tuned by love. Every atom in your body is listening, remembering, waiting to be heard. And all of this is not fantasy—it is the physics of how your soul translates itself into the fields of the physical.

THE HOLOGRAPHIC BODY NETWORK

As mentioned, leading-edge neuroscience has proven the existence of microtubules extending from our brain's dendritic cells, nanofibers operating like quantum antennae capable of accessing subatomic data. From the perspective of my theories, these microtubules are simply the smallest forms of biological antennae, structurally allowing the passage of information from entangled protons all the way up to the level of our nervous system, neural networks, and physiology as a whole.

If all the protons in the body are in constant information exchange with our surroundings (and really, anyone and anything, anywhere in the universe), then our brains are like recorders, translating the quantum field state of our experience into cellular structures and neural networks, attempting to build an internal biological hologram of the external experiences we're having.

We only access small amounts of this information consciously, but these simple scientific realizations reveal how it is possible to experience the entire universe as your body, just as many avatars and spiritual masters describe, and as I have personally had the joy of experiencing many times in my life.

Since the protons throughout the universe have been storing every moment of their existence, it becomes obvious that we can connect to any location in the present moment and access information about almost any location at any time in the past. The question is, how much of that information do we have access to, and what are the mechanisms for retrieval?

From a practical standpoint, you might already have considered that the actual bits of data in each proton would not reveal much by themselves. If you look at any small group of bits on a computer, it may be impossible to discern what kind of data is being composed. However, when you have large amounts of bits in the kilobyte (thousands), megabyte (millions), or gigabyte (billions) range, we can render entire files, images, and videos on our computers. The level of data stored in a complete and comprehensive physical memory is vaster than even the most high-definition video.

SECRETS IN STONE

It's also important to consider that most materials decompose and the protons that were once in any object end up scattered in dust, washed away by rain, and returned to the ocean or atmosphere. What kind of objects would have a consistent set of protons over thousands or millions of years, enabling a massive, networked set of data to exist, potentially capable of being accessed?

Megaliths.

While most materials degrade, disperse, or are consumed by entropy, certain stones, particularly dense crystalline structures like granite, basalt, and obsidian, retain their atomic integrity across millennia. Protons within these stones remain largely undisturbed for thousands, even millions of years, quietly holding the quantum imprint of everything that touches them. Like ancient monks in deep meditation, they sit still, recording.

It is no accident that the oldest sacred sites on Earth are built from these materials. The megaliths of Earth are not merely architectural marvels; they are memory temples.

Unexplained giant stone structures form the basis of many of the most ancient sites on Earth, and many archaeologists and researchers now believe that these sites were constructed before the global cataclysm and flood at the end of the last Ice Age, known as the Younger Dryas, nearly 13,000 years ago.

Mainstream academic sources still refuse to accept these "ancient apocalypse" theories. In contrast, their common academic explanations for the methods and timelines of construction of these sites are often ridiculed by engineers and physicists who understand what it would take to build these structures. The reality is that you can't break or carve a stone with a hardness of 9.5 on the Mohs Hardness Scale with a copper hammer and chisel. The inconceivable precision of stone cutting and placements in sites like the Serapeum and the famous Great Pyramid of Giza in Egypt, Ollantaytambo in Peru, and countless other sites around the world would require far more advanced technology than was available in the commonly accepted archeological timeline.

What if these massive stones were used for more than architectural construction and were intended to provide information and memory banks of information for future observers? Consider that the Ancient Egyptians, Incans, Mayans, peoples across Southeast Asia, and Native Americans all carved records of their histories into stone.

Megalithic structures such as mysterious pyramids and enormous foundation stones under temples around the world, the precision-cut stones of Puma Punku in Bolivia, the serpentine alignments of Carnac in France, the Serapeum, and the gravity-defying walls of Ollantaytambo are not simply relics of a forgotten technology. They are repositories. Memory engines. Quantum temples of the Ancients. Hard drives encoded with ceremony, starlight, resonance, and intent; vibrational archives of living memory. Every step of their construction, every chant, every solar alignment was a ritual act of programming the memory field of stone.

INDIGENOUS TRADITIONS AND THE ANCIENT PAST

Many indigenous traditions still carry this truth. The Lakota speak to the Stone People as the eldest Grandfathers, keepers of time. Inipi ceremonies—sweat lodges—are held not just to cleanse the body, but to awaken the stones' memory and call forth ancestral teachings through steam and silence. The Cherokee, too, speak of stones as living witnesses, and the Kogi of Colombia refer to sacred rocks as *Aluna* vessels, storing spiritual essence to be read by the Mamas, their high priests.

But perhaps the most provocative realization emerges when we bridge this living wisdom with the possibility of Atlantean technology. If, as the myths and mysterious memories of so many people suggest, Atlantis was a civilization deeply attuned to the geometry of spacetime and the quantum structure of matter, then it would follow that they developed memory technologies far beyond anything we possess today using megaliths as vast energetic hard drives, programmable through harmonic frequencies, crystalline resonance, and magnetic alignment.

Each standing stone may not only mark a celestial event, it may be an energetic capacitor, receiving and broadcasting subtle informational fields. A library not of books, but of being.

GATES OF MEMORY

Now consider, what if these stones weren't merely memorials of ancient rites, but tools to restore memory in the present? Could it be that touching a megalith with reverent awareness activates a resonance between your own protonic lattice and the records stored in its crystalline body? Could such contact reawaken soul memories that lie dormant in your field, encoded in the vacuum, waiting for harmonic activation?

For me, the answer is yes. Exploring Egypt reawakened my lifetimes there, but not just because I visited sites. I learned to sing to the stones, to feel their memory and resonance, and they reawakened my own. I've experienced the same across ancient sacred sites in Mexico. The Stone Circles of the British Isles are calling to me again, like a long-lost lover singing my way home.

In this light, past life recall is not only internal, but also environmental. It is encoded in the spaces we walk, the objects we touch, and the stones we stand upon and sing beside. The Earth herself is a planetary memory field, and we are participants in the act of remembering Her.

These insights suggest that you are not a passive traveler through time; You are a living archive, encoded with the echoes of stars and lifetimes past. You are composed of quantum instruments, protons, atoms, and cells, all built upon memory fields stretching back to the beginning of time. Every part of you can remember, when tuned correctly.

This journey into past lives is not a regression; it is a *restoration,* a re-tuning of your awareness to the full scale of your being.

The soul remembers.

The stones remember.

And now, so will you.

SOUL JOURNEYS AND
SPIRITUAL GROWTH

*W*e remember our past lives for a reason. It is not simply to be enchanted by fragments of other times or to indulge in stories of who we might have been, but to heal, to grow, to evolve.

When we begin to access past life memory, what we're truly doing is opening a larger window into the soul's journey. We are lifting the veil on our own curriculum, the unique path our soul has walked across time to gather wisdom, to resolve karma, to cultivate gifts, and to deepen its capacity for love and service.

It is through this larger view that true healing begins. The pains that seem inexplicable in this lifetime, from unshakable fears, recurring relationship patterns, emotional loops, or even physical ailments, often reveal themselves to be echoes of unresolved experiences carried forward through the incarnational arc. To remember is to interrupt that pattern, to bring consciousness to what has been unconscious, and in doing so, to liberate the energy that was once trapped in an unprocessed story.

This is not merely about psychological integration. It is a sacred process of spiritual alchemy.

Many ancient traditions speak of the soul's evolution through multiple lifetimes. From the Buddhist wheel of Samsara to the Vedic understanding of karma and dharma, from the Egyptian weighing of the heart to the mystery schools of Greece, the idea that our lives are sequentially linked in cause, effect, and transformation has been encoded in humanity's spiritual DNA since the beginning.

While some modern spiritual teachings suggest that all lifetimes are happening simultaneously, it is important to distinguish between the energetic resonance of multiple lifetimes (which can be accessed non-linearly) and the actual sequence of soul experience. Healing a wound in this life may affect how you relate to similar patterns that echo through time, but it does not rewrite the literal past. Our soul's journey unfolds through experience, integration, and evolution, and this process inherently requires a linear sequence. You cannot integrate a future lesson before the prior wound has occurred, nor can you embody the wisdom of a life that has not yet been lived. Even within a transdimensional soul perspective, the architecture of healing still honors chronology as a scaffolding for coherence.

Reincarnation is not simply a system of rebirth; it is a learning engine. Through different lives, we experience different roles: student and teacher, perpetrator and healer, king and servant, betrayer and betrayed. These lives are not random. They are curated by the soul, sometimes in response to choices made, sometimes in collaboration with other souls. Each incarnation becomes a stage in a greater story of becoming.

This is where the concept of karmic patterns becomes more than a mystical notion. Karma is not punishment; it is unfinished energy, an invitation for balance. If we leave a lifetime with unresolved harm, guilt, or a lack of understanding, we often draw similar circumstances again, to provide the opportunity to respond differently. Likewise, if we die with unexpressed gifts or unfulfilled purpose, the soul often brings those threads back to the next life, waiting for the right moment to bloom.

Remembering a past life where you were silenced may explain why you've struggled to speak up in this one. A pattern of abandonment might trace back to vows made centuries ago in grief or devotion. Sometimes even deep phobias around fire, water, heights, confinement, and countless other conditions aren't rooted in childhood trauma, but in echoes from lifetimes past.

When these patterns become conscious, they become malleable. And this is where the work of past life integration becomes a path of deep soul liberation.

Yet this journey doesn't end with healing. Past life recall also reawakens gifts, wisdom, and skills. Many people discover talents that were cultivated over many lifetimes, such as medicine, music, language, calligraphy, leadership, and spiritual practices. These are not random aptitudes. They are soul skills, carried across time, waiting to be reactivated.

Remembering who we have been helps us claim who we are now, and it gives us clarity on who we are becoming.

The idea of life purpose becomes far less abstract when we understand it in this light. It is not a fixed career or role; it is a trajectory of soul development. Your soul may have returned in this life to complete something it began long ago, to resolve a conflict, redeem a relationship, or bring forward wisdom once lost. Your passions, gifts, and even your greatest challenges may all be clues to your incarnational mission.

Some souls return with a singular focus: to serve, to protect, to heal. Others return as bridge-builders, bringing forward forgotten knowledge or preparing the ground for future awakenings. The deeper we look, the more coherent the picture becomes. We are not wandering blindly through lifetimes. We are learning to remember, to refine, and to realize our Divine potential.

And how is all of this carried forward? How does the soul's memory thread itself into form again and again?

Here we return to the body, and to our own DNA.

As mentioned in an earlier chapter, a vast percentage of human DNA is still considered non-coding by mainstream science. Often labeled as "junk DNA," this mysterious territory may be anything but. What if it is here that the records of our soul journey are encoded, not just the genetics of our ancestors, but the experiences of our own past selves?

Quantum biology, epigenetics, and biophysics all suggest that DNA is far more dynamic than previously understood. Researchers have observed how energetic states, trauma, belief, and intention can influence gene expression, turning certain sequences on or off. Our DNA is not a static code, it is a responsive, living archive.

If soul experience is woven into our genetics, either as vibrational imprint, quantum information, or energetic architecture, then past life memory is not just a metaphysical phenomenon. It is biological, embodied, and accessible.

Perhaps more importantly, it is transformable.

We now know that emotional healing, somatic integration, and spiritual practice can change not just our minds and behaviors, but potentially, the very code we pass on. When we transmute trauma, reclaim lost gifts, and realign with our soul's purpose, we may be changing what we leave behind genetically. This is how soul work becomes ancestral repair. It's not only that we carry the wounds of those who came before us, we carry the keys to their liberation, and ours.

And yet, for many of us, the process of accessing our past lives can sometimes lead to a sense of fragmentation. We begin to remember lifetimes in which we played radically different roles, expressing different personalities, belief systems, genders, and orientations, dramatically shifting many key aspects of ourselves from life to life. At first, this diversity can feel disorienting or even overwhelming.

Who am I, really, if I have been all these different versions of self?

Yet this question is not a crisis, it is the threshold of wholeness.

Each facet of your soul that arises from a past life is not a separate identity to get lost in; instead, it is a key. A gift. A thread of truth. And when we focus only on one thread or get caught up in the glamour or trauma of a specific incarnation, we risk losing our grounding in the present. We begin to act from memory instead of mastery.

Integration is the sacred act of bringing all those pieces home, of honoring every lifetime not as a detour, but as a deliberate expression of your soul's vast spectrum. The warrior, the healer, the artist, the priestess, the rebel, the mystic; these are all within you now. Not in conflict, but in council.

As you gather the pieces and weave them together, you begin to feel more whole in this life. This is not just because you've accessed more memories, but because you've integrated and become more of yourself. Past life integration reveals the deeper architecture of the soul, and with it, a profound sense of inner coherence. The many become one. The fragments become a fabric.

The magic lies in the realization that your life is not an isolated chapter. It is a thread in a vast tapestry of becoming. And you are both the weaver and the woven.

As you remember, you change. As you heal, you upgrade the very code of your being.

And as you live with awareness, the future generations of your family, your species, and your soul lineage, are blessed with new possibilities.

We are not just inheritors of the past. We are architects of the future.

And every memory reclaimed is a doorway into the becoming of something far greater than we've ever known.

SOUL FAMILIES AND SOUL CONTRACTS

here is something unmistakable about certain people we meet, those who feel instantly familiar, whose presence cracks open something ancient inside of us. A gaze that softens the armor, a laugh that echoes from lifetimes past; these are not accidents. They are reunions.

As we explore the deeper nature of the soul's journey, it becomes clear that we are not traveling alone. We incarnate again and again within constellations of other souls, which many traditions and spiritual systems refer to as *soul families*. These are souls with whom we share profound bonds, unfinished stories, deep karmic entanglements, or sacred missions.

Your soul family includes the ones who have challenged you, healed you, betrayed you, adored you, and walked beside you through the fire of transformation. Sometimes they appear as parents, lovers, mentors, or friends. Sometimes they return as rivals, antagonists, or even enemies, because that is the role needed for your growth. The soul does not prioritize comfort. It prioritizes evolution.

And evolution is rarely linear. It moves in spirals, in echoes, in repeating patterns. That's where the concept of soul contracts comes into view.

Before we incarnate, we often make agreements with other souls: contracts crafted in love, sometimes in pain, often in deep purpose. These agreements shape the architecture of our incarnations. They form the energetic blueprints of the relationships that we enter: deep and unshakable trust, profound love, and the joy of family, but also the lessons we must face, wounds we must heal, and forgiveness we must embody.

These contracts are not always easy. They may bind us to people who bring us heartbreak or confusion, only for us to learn boundaries, self-worth, or compassion. Others may carry the sweetness of reunion, the unmistakable pull of a soul we've loved across lifetimes. These are the ones who arrive and feel like home, even if the story doesn't last forever. Every soul contract is a thread in the larger weave.

Over the years, I have uncovered many such contracts in my own life. Some of the most powerful relationships I've had were not new, they were ancient. I've felt the joy of reuniting with kindred spirits, the pain of unfinished love, and the bittersweet ache of finding someone again only to realize that our paths diverged for a reason. I have known the greatest joys and sorrows imaginable. Yet I have also discovered one thing above all. Love is the ultimate answer to every question, every quest, every epic tale in time. Through remembering past lives, I've been able to heal what once felt impossible. Rage has turned to understanding. Fear has softened into forgiveness. The impossible becomes sacred when we understand its purpose and learn how to accept and love ourselves.

Our current relationships are rarely as simple as they seem. Past life connections often lie beneath the surface, influencing the dynamics we face now. That recurring conflict with a family member, the unspoken bond with a friend, the magnetic pull to someone who feels like destiny, all of these experiences may have roots in lifetimes long past.

Sometimes, just remembering that deeper connection is enough to shift the energy. But other times, healing requires intentional work: regression, inner journeying, soul retrieval, forgiveness rituals. We can resolve karmic patterns across lifetimes by bringing awareness, compassion, and choice to the present moment.

And this is the key: Soul contracts are not cages. They are invitations. They are not punishments, but sacred opportunities. And while they may guide us, they do not enslave us. As we grow in awareness, we also grow in sovereignty. We can choose to complete certain contracts. We can rewrite the terms. We can even release those that no longer serve our evolution. We will cover how to do this in later chapters.

Each of these opportunities represents a choice. We've made many choices in the past, writing contracts through our oaths and commitments. Now, in this moment, we have the potential to make new choices. We can choose to clear and remove, cancel, and resolve old agreements simply by stating what we are choosing to clear with passion and focused intention. We can witness the dissolution of old energies and bindings by simply commanding that they be dissolved and our energy bodies restored to their highest and best state.

This is part of why exploring past lives can be so powerful: We come into clarity and understanding around the agreements we've made in the past, and we have an opportunity to change, heal, and receive the truth about who we truly are and why we have the experiences we have.

What becomes stunningly clear, as we open to these truths, is that we are part of a vast network of souls, each weaving in and out of each other's lives like dancers in a sacred play. Some are with us every incarnation. Others join for a time and then drift away, only to return lifetimes later in new form or new costume with the same essence. All of us, in one way or another, are bound by love.

And this weaving is not limited to Earth.

Some of our soul family extends beyond this world. Across star systems, galaxies, and even other planes of existence. We are part of a greater soul lineage, what some call "star families." While many of these beings incarnate physically just like us, others are not in physical bodies, but their presence is no less real. They may be strongly felt on the *astral plane*, known as the mental plane in esoteric traditions, or even down to the *etheric plane*, often referred to as the emotional or frequency-based plane of existence, which is close enough to the physical world to influence electrical and quantum fields.

They may also whisper in dreams, arrive in synchronicities, and reveal themselves through resonance alone as a feeling or deep knowing that permeates the space near you.

The love we feel that transcends time and form may not come from just one lifetime. It may come from hundreds or thousands, from other civilizations or other dimensions. We are eternal beings playing in the finite. And every person you've ever loved, you may yet come to love again.

As your sense of self expands beyond the personal, so does your capacity to hold others in a greater field of compassion. You begin to see not just who people are now, but who they've been, and who you have been, and have become, together. From that recognition comes a deep peace, and sometimes a kind of soul ecstasy, when the reunion is recognized consciously.

This chapter of your journey is an invitation to reflect: Whom do you feel you've known before? Where in your life is there an unfinished story? Where is there deep resonance… or deep resistance?

These questions are not for the mind to answer alone. Let your soul speak. Let your body feel. Let memory rise where it will and know that the web you're a part of is vast, beautiful, and alive.

We are not here to walk alone. We are here to remember, together. And in that remembrance, we find the ancient agreements and the power to make new ones.

Because the soul is not a solitary traveler. It is a constellation. A chorus. A family of light that never stops calling us home.

LIVES ACROSS THE UNIVERSE

W hat does it mean to live many lives, not just on this Earth, but across worlds, cultures, dimensions, and civilizations that stretch beyond human memory? The soul is not limited to the arc of a single planetary incarnation. It journeys through realms, weaving its essence into the fabric of many timelines and worlds.

Let us begin where we are now: Earth.

On this planet alone, there are endless forms of incarnation. A soul may live as a healer in a rural village, a philosopher in a golden temple, a mother in a war-torn land, or a leader of nations. We may experience lifetimes of poverty and lifetimes of privilege, each carrying lessons and opportunities for growth. The diversity of Earth's expressions, from cultural to emotional and environmental, provides a kind of spiritual crucible. Earth incarnation is a school of intense polarity and accelerated evolution. The emotional density here gives each experience a unique poignancy.

For many, Earth is a kind of training ground. The compression of time, the interplay of free will and consequence, and the soul's capacity to forget— and then remember—make this world a powerful place of refinement. But Earth is not the only place a soul may incarnate.

Beyond this world, there are countless civilizations where souls choose to live and learn. Some of these are planetary, like Earth, while others may be interdimensional hubs, consciousness-based collectives, or advanced societies with technologies that blur the line between spirit and science. On such worlds, souls may incarnate into highly cooperative collectives, serve as planetary stewards, or participate in star-faring civilizations where the interface between energy, frequency, and form is well understood.

These galactic lifetimes can be profoundly different from Earth incarnations. On worlds where memory is preserved between lives, the soul may build on its knowledge consciously, evolving in spirals of coherence and service. Roles taken in such lifetimes may include harmonic engineers, planetary diplomats, frequency navigators, energy architects, and guardians of interdimensional thresholds. In some civilizations, children are trained from a young age to tune their bodies to different harmonic states, to interface with crystalline libraries, or to commune with star intelligences. These lifetimes may feel fantastical to the Earth-bound mind, yet to the soul, they are simply part of its tapestry.

Many people carry faint echoes of such galactic lives. These surface as unexplained memories of floating in starlit chambers, speaking telepathically, or working with light-based technologies. Others feel drawn to the stars without knowing why, sensing a home they cannot locate in space but feel deeply in their bones.

TYPES OF MEMORY

As our memories across lifetimes begin to surface, one of the challenges we face is distinguishing between archetypal resonance and personal experience. It is essential for the *chronomancer*, the time-traveling past life explorer, to understand the difference between archetypal and visceral memory.

It is common for someone to begin accessing a past life memory by recognizing figures they were near in a previous life who have modern mythological or historical significance. A person may feel an intense resonance with a powerful being from the past, such as a spiritual teacher, a king, a warrior, or a cultural hero. But often, the soul did not embody that figure—it orbited close to them, as someone who met them or knew them well. Our first glimpses into past lives are often activated by these larger-than-life characters because they hold strong energetic signatures. Yet the truth of our own role is often quieter, more personal, more complex.

Visceral memories, by contrast, are those that arrive with unmistakable emotional and sensory clarity. They may come in dreams, flashbacks, or through the presence of someone we've known before. These memories are often triggered by profound emotional events: loss, love, betrayal, and triumph. They can be so specific that they arrive with tastes, sounds, and scents. We might not recall the whole story, but we remember a moment. And through that moment, a whole lifetime can begin to unfold when we begin to shine the light of our awareness into experiences before and after that moment.

My own path has been one of gradually layering these insights. In my book *The Dragon Key*, I recount the journey of remembering many shared lives with a soul companion named Rastara. Through our interactions with others who also shared those lives, more and more pieces came into view. Our roles clarified, our experiences deepened, and new gifts awakened. Where I once saw her as a lover, I discovered her as a sister. Where I once saw her as a life partner, I recognized her as a rite of passage. Where I once thought of her as a twin flame, I discovered her as a partner in a soul contract to travel to Earth together.

At times, we would discover that archetypes we carried in this life had echoes in others, as ambassadors, guardians, and beloveds. Each time a key was revealed, the tapestry of my self-awareness became more vivid, more whole.

Then, sometimes in our deep personal awakening to our past, the story remembered is not just personal—it is famous. You may find your memories reveal an alignment with the stories about someone known to history. While this can be exciting, it can also bring unexpected weight. The truth is, remembering a powerful past life does not make your path easier. It requires deep humility to carry that memory without ego. We must be willing to remember for our own wholeness, not to gain admiration or status. When we integrate these parts of ourselves with reverence and responsibility, something luminous happens: People begin to feel that truth emanate from within us, without us ever needing to say a word.

Now that we have explored the power and potency of accessing individual visceral memories and understanding archetypal resonance, we can also look at ancestral memories. Let's review all three to compare and contrast them in simple terms.

Individual memory is the first-person experience of a lifetime your soul has lived. These visceral memories often carry emotional intensity and may include vivid moments of recognition when meeting someone again or visiting a place for the first time that feels like home.

Archetypal resonance, on the other hand, connects us to larger fields of symbolic energy. We may resonate deeply with a figure like Alexander the Great, Mary Magdalene, or Quetzalcoatl, not because we were them but because our soul has worked in alignment with that archetype, carried similar frequencies in parallel roles, or experienced them personally through an adjacent incarnation where we were near them in the same time period. These connections can reveal qualities we are meant to embody, but they are not direct lifetimes.

Ancestral memory, meanwhile, is woven through our bloodline. These impressions may emerge as inherited trauma, recurring dreams, or behavioral patterns that do not stem from our own experience. Unlike past life memories, ancestral memories are not held in the soul's direct experiential field, but in the genetic and epigenetic patterns passed down through our lineage. These memories are often more subtle and take the form of emotional habits, health patterns, or unconscious fears, yet they offer profound healing when brought into consciousness.

As we begin to decode the strands of these memories, we find that there are common roles we tend to play across lifetimes. These are soul preferences and the echoes of ancient callings.

Some of us return as warriors, protectors, or defenders of sacred truth. Others come as weavers, dreamers, and healers, souls that shape the fabric of culture and community. There are those who walk the path of the magician, alchemist, or priestess, bridging spirit and matter, holding temples of remembrance across time. And still others are diplomats, explorers, and *star walkers*, those who travel between worlds, building bridges across cultures and dimensions.

As we explore the commonalities between lives, we begin to see the deeper architecture of our soul. We discover the continuity of essence across the diversity of roles, the unique way our soul moves through lifetimes, returning again to certain truths, callings, and joys.

TYPES OF BEINGS AND STAR FAMILIES

Beyond the archetypes and patterns woven through earthly lives, there are deeper mysteries. Many of our soul threads extend far beyond this planet, into relationships with other worlds, star systems, and dimensional realities. These are not just myths or channeled curiosities. For many of us, they are soul truths remembered in dreams, visions, or the sudden knowing that home is not entirely here.

As past life memories awaken, some people begin to recall lifetimes that didn't happen on Earth at all. They remember starships, crystalline cities, spherical classrooms of light, and worlds with dual suns and living architecture. They remember being part of civilizations where travel between stars was as common as sailing between islands on Earth. These memories may come in flashes, through deep soul resonance, or through contact experiences that activate cellular remembrance.

Among the most common star families recalled by souls incarnated on Earth are the Sirians, Pleiadians, Arcturians, Lyrans, and Andromedans. Each carries a distinct energetic frequency and evolutionary arc. Yet there are many more species out there, some that look similar to humans and are the source of some of our genetics, and others that look vastly different.

Sirians are often remembered as Elven guardians of ancient wisdom, singers of the seals and gates between worlds, builders of forest cities and waterfall temples, and healers who work with light, sound, elementals, and planetary grids. The ancient Irish and Celtic bloodlines carry strong Sirian signatures, and many of these lineages are thought to have originated with the Tuatha De Danann, who arrived in the British Isles *"riding clouds, blocking out the skies for three days and nights, and bringing with them four sacred treasures from islands in the sky."*

Pleiadians all learned to sing to the waters, commune with dolphins and cetaceans, and find their own path through life. They tend to be extremely emotionally intelligent, artistic, and relationally focused on a core level, often guiding humanity's emotional healing. Their root bloodlines are often seen in Polynesian, Southeast Asian, and Nordic lineages, but they have incarnated into nearly every culture on Earth as ambassadors and bridge-builders between peoples.

Arcturians are master architects of stone and memory systems, advanced mathematicians, ancestral cartographers, and geneticists. They bring many forms of technological mastery, including frequency healing, often through facing the darkness and awakening light. They also excel in architectural design on both the energetic and structural planes. They often have secret missions in each incarnation, hiding key facets of their own awareness from themselves until specific junctures when these astral or mental shields unlock. Their bloodlines are rooted across indigenous Native American, Jewish, and Egyptian lineages, but they also incarnate in many other genetic families.

Shihaelei, from the Betelgeuse region of the Orion star system, are innately artists of movement and action, the ancient secret roots of the Samurai archetype and many Asian lineages on Earth. They often incarnate as warriors, martial artists, monks, and members of special forces units. Those who have integrated this soul lineage well are often guardians of peace, channeling abilities with weapons and movement into fire performances and flow arts, and their physical ability into protective fields and securing sovereignty.

Yahonians are medicine-keepers from a jungle planet in a star system near the chest of the Draco constellation, near what we call Epsilon Draconis. They speak the language of plants and teach how every plant provides an energetic balance to our bodies, minds, and spirits. They often incarnated into African and Amazonian bloodlines on Earth, along with some central European bloodlines like Moldovans.

Lyrans are ancestral pioneers, often taking feline humanoid embodiments or carrying the sacred covenant of the Tiara Danan, a female fleet of guardians who protect worlds and artifacts. The star systems of Lyra give rise to bold, creative, and passionate beings, often involved in the original seeding of many worlds, including Earth.

Andromedans is a broad term that may refer to local star systems in the Andromeda constellation or systems in the nearby Andromeda Galaxy. Our local Andromedans in the Milky Way carry advanced evolutionary perspectives and often serve as cosmic diplomats, bridging realities beyond time and space. Various species thought to originate in the Andromeda Galaxy include dragons, humanoid elephants (like Ganesha and Appa), and many avian races.

Zeta Reticuli, are often referred to as the "Greys." This species has various heights and appearances, though we mostly only see them through the stereotypical "alien" lens that has been well-propagated by disinformation campaigns to hide the actual nature of our contact with these beings on Earth. The Zetas are powerfully telepathic and often have used embedded chips and devices to augment this ability. They commonly think in hive minds, a result of the programming forcing them to link minds as assault units during the Orion Wars, similar to stormtroopers in the *Star Wars* films. They have been healing from this programming since then, and through creating soul contracts, they have incarnated as humans many times, often then "abducting" their own people to study humanity's powerful emotional and biological characteristics.

Other beings remembered include the **Nguura, LaQuinon**, and the **Zai'Ten**—names that may not be found in books but are known through direct remembrance and deep soul lineage work.

Many souls also recall a vast array of non-humanoid forms: crystalline intelligences, serpentine energy beings, luminous winged species, aquatic empaths, and even radiant energy collectives with no fixed form. These beings may appear alien to the mind, yet familiar to the heart. Some of them remember visceral physical embodiments while others feel as though they were energetic forms, souls incarnated into causal, astral, and etheric bodies, but not physical ones.

In my own work with the Galactic Family, I've seen repeatedly how people begin to unlock these soul lineages not through external seeking, but through deep internal resonance. A color, a frequency, a geometric vision, a name whispered in meditation—these open doors. And as we walk through them, we begin to see ourselves not just as visitors to Earth, but as emissaries, pilgrims, or bridge-keepers between dimensions.

PARALLEL MULTIVERSE OR CAUSAL CONTINUUM?

Every soul seeker eventually comes to question the nature of time and whether we live parallel lives in addition to this multidimensional existence.

Recent quantum mechanical experiments have shown strange things about time. At least on the information level, data seems to be able to flow back and forth through time, appearing to break linear chronology and the general idea of cause and effect.

This has spawned countless ideas about multiple timelines, including that every moment could split into an infinite number of branches of different universes or timelines and speculating that these branches run parallel to our own.

Due to many splashy articles about this potential infinite multiverse, it has become popular in some circles to speak of living simultaneous lives in parallel universes as other "yous" having different experiences in different timelines. While this idea has metaphorical and astral truth, there are important distinctions to understand.

CONSIDER THIS

Imagine there is another version of you in a separate parallel timeline, and this part of you grew up with entirely different experiences, relationships, choices, events, and connections.

Will that version of you ever become who you are now?

No.

Will you ever remember or integrate all of this parallel timeline's experiences?

No.

Therefore, while this can be an interesting mental or astral exercise, there is nothing that suggests that this alternate version of you, or parallel timeline, exists in any physical sense. In addition, one can easily become lost in considering alternate versions of self. Many people with significant psychological issues attempt to rewrite their past, convincing themselves that something else happened, creating a story in their minds that does not match the actual flow of events in physical reality.

In ancient metaphysical traditions, this is resolved at the level of the *causal plane*, which is said to exist above and encompasses the mental or astral plane. At this level, our lives are understood in the terms of a causal universe, where time unfolds through relationship, learning, and resolution, and our souls follow a coherent thread. We may explore many potentials, yes, but not all are as literal lives being lived simultaneously in physicality. Rather, what we often encounter in dreams or altered states are *simulacra*, constructs of possibility that help us understand our options, heal fragments, or integrate unresolved energy.

True soul incarnation is relational. It is woven through bonds, lessons, and co-creation with others. This is why we do not need to be overwhelmed by the idea of infinite versions of ourselves. There is great joy in realizing that we've already lived what we needed to live, and we may find perfection, or sometimes profound meaning, in accepting it. We do not need to carry the burden of infinite parallel trauma. We are whole in our trajectory and complete in our spiral. And we are free to choose, now and always.

MULTIDIMENSIONAL EXPERIENCE

It is important to recognize that the soul is not confined to either the physical or mental plane. Across each of our higher dimensions of experience—etheric, astral, causal, akashic, atmic or buddha, and even the celestial—we often have aspects of ourselves active. These are not separate people, but expressions of the levels of consciousness of our multidimensional being, working in harmony to evolve the whole. These higher-self aspects guide, nudge, and hold memory while we navigate Earth's density.

Many occult traditions suggest that when we face untenable challenges on one level of our experience, the solution can often be found by viewing that experience from a higher plane of existence. Here's a series of examples that exemplify this process and how you can use it yourself to transcend difficulties and resolve seemingly impossible problems:

1. You have a chronic physical condition and doctors can't figure out what is going on. You've tried all types of Western medical help, but the side effects of the pharmaceutical drugs are causing other problems. This is a perfect time to begin exploring the etheric plane and your emotional body. Visit an acupuncturist who works with the etheric field through five-element theory. Try receiving Reiki or visiting an energy healer. Do emotional rituals to release stuck feelings in the body.

2. Emotions are overwhelming to you and you consistently have anxiety or you can't seem to get a handle on your feelings. Refine your skills on the mental plane, above the etheric, and question your

beliefs and self-talk. Work to understand the connections between different events or experiences and the feelings you have. Create new frameworks for safety, self-acceptance, and validation in your mind to redefine your views about yourself.

3. Mentally, you're in chaos. Your mind is part bucking bronco and part bull, drawn to every red flag. You've split your attention across a hundred projects and see a thousand different versions of you across timelines. You don't really know who you are because your mind can't settle on what defines you as an individual. This is a key time to transcend the mental plane and its astral impressions and focus on the causal plane of your relationships. Meditate on the connections and relationships you've had throughout your life. Remember the connections that made you feel deeply at home in yourself. Spend time reconnecting with friends and loved ones and ask them what they see in you. Rediscover the potential and magic of the field of relationships that have forged you into the person you are now.

4. You're obsessed with what people think or feel about you. Your relational field has become overbearing, and you feel stuck and overly defined by other people's perspectives. Ascend into your awareness of the Akashic plane and do past life practice and recall. By discovering who you are beyond this life, you restore a deeper fundamental awareness of yourself and expand the context of the causal relationships that help define your identity.

5. After exploring many lifetimes and integrating them, you begin to over-identify with a specific lifetime or role and inadvertently begin expecting others to treat you as though you are that person. Now is the time to practice accessing the atmic plane, above the akasha, meditating on the reality that across all time, you and others have played all possible roles. At this level you are practicing true humility and witnessing the truth behind the paradox of individuality and

oneness. Here you can begin to clearly experience the divinity in others.

6. When fully experiencing atmic plane consciousness, there are very few challenges that remain in experience. Yet sometimes a high initiate at this level still feels some sense of being separate from their Divinity, an output of creation rather than Creator. Through deep soul longing for union with the infinite, eternal Source of all love, one begins to experience the celestial plane directly, where the self can experience their full Divine nature and also still play across the realms of differentiation.

As we awaken, we begin to integrate not only our past lives but our higher-dimensional selves. Some would call this process ascension, and yet inevitably, the higher we go in perspective, the more important it is to reintegrate those realizations back down through our mental, emotional, and physical layers of experience. This is the real meaning of *embodiment*: bringing all layers of our being into coherence here and now.

And so, we return to this: the sacred responsibility of focus in this lifetime.

For all the soul's grandeur, for all the stars we remember and dimensions we touch, it is this body, this breath, this Earth that is calling for our presence. The goal is not to escape this life through memory or vision, but to become more fully alive within it. Past lives are not detours; they are nutrients. And the star families we recall are not destinations; they are mirrors reminding us of who we truly are.

You are not here by accident. You are a culmination of stories, star fire, and soul vows. But you are also this breath. This choice. This moment.

The deeper we go into our memories, the more we must return to presence, because it is here that we integrate. It is here that we transform and here that we love, serve, and evolve.

And that is the great paradox of soul work. That we travel through galaxies... to return more fully to ourselves. We remember countless lifetimes... to be more present in this one. And we touch the stars... only to bring their light home, to Earth.

PART TWO

Spiritual Explorations of Earth and Galactic Past Lives

People forget their lives from one birth to the next, but the soul never forgets. Memory lives not in the mind, but in the being.

— LAO TZU

THE TALE OF TADANAGA

The art of movement, the drawing of a sword, the presence of a Master, the secret powers hidden within martial forms—these always intrigued me, even as a child. I found myself practicing martial arts and dance since my earliest memories and developed skill quickly in every form I tried.

My body became my proof that I was strong and that I had power, simply through how I could move. My movement was the validation that gave me confidence, even when my thin, lanky body felt judged in comparison to the male ideal.

When I got old enough to use chopsticks, they were immediately familiar. When I held my first swords, I felt my entire body shift and I knew exactly how to use them. Yet nothing quite prepared me for the first time I drew a Katana from its sheath.

My stance shifted, left foot back and at forty-five degrees, my front leg aiming, my body relaxing completely as I held the tsuka (handle) softly with my right hand, and gripped the *saya* (scabbard) near the top with my left.

As I became a still pool of water, my body felt like a lake held behind a dam and I looked in the direction of my draw. I knew that I could instantly reach anything within ten feet in that general direction, leaping off my back foot while drawing the sword and striking upward and to the right with a single movement. I felt it, and I knew it.

That first draw, I didn't leap, but as I slid the sword forth in a rising arc of lightning, I could feel all the ways the blade wanted to move from there. It wanted to fall like a shooting star, rise like the sun, slice through the reeds, strike like a bolt from the sky, and dance among the bamboo. I let my mind go, and my body just…moved.

I felt the cool air on the hard stones of old courtyards and smelled the sweet, delicate blooms of the falling cherry blossoms. Then I was inside a wooden *dojo*, its pillars inscribed with ancient wisdom passed down through generations, my feet firmly sticking to smooth but textured bamboo flooring. I danced the sword with a young woman who laughed even as her eyes flared with intensity and I found myself defending against a master whose movements were as quick as a hornet and more fluid than a tea ceremony.

These layers of memories came as easily as the movements of my body through forms and my body surged with energy and familiarity.

That first glimpse was just the beginning. Some years later, while I was in college, I looked across the grassy fields in the center of campus and saw Rastara, a woman I had already been having flashbacks and memories with…but mostly from the Middle Ages. Suddenly, everything shifted in my perception, and I was looking at a Japanese woman carrying a basket on her head as she walked into a thatch-roofed village.

I stood at the edge of a forest, eyes peering through the holes of a mask, my breath warm within it. I could feel the armor laced across my body and the katana and wakizashi strapped around my waist. My right hand held the reins of a horse behind me, and I knew she had a dark midnight coat under her armor and saddles, but I could not tear my eyes from the woman.

She was going home, where she would be beaten and abused again by the man who had bought her. I had seen her dance many times, years before when she was a *geisha* who served my family. Some part of me ached for her and loved her so much that it was irrational. Now she was in a house of pain and all I could feel was the surge of rage and intensity to end it.

That was about all I remembered at that moment, but both she and I continued to feel the layers of our Japanese connection unfolding through subtle hints, synchronicities, and movies we loved. We felt every heart-throbbing layer of stories like *Memories of a Geisha* and *Crouching Tiger, Hidden Dragon*. The feelings and familiarity were unmistakable.

In the year following these glimpses, a few soul brothers and I decided to create an underground event venue where we could throw parties, raise money, produce music, and bring together community. It was called CORE, and we had many acronyms for it, including Consciously Organized Resonant Essence.

One of these brothers and I decided to do a sword performance together at one of the parties, dancing live blades (fully sharp) between belly dancers. One of the dancers was Rastara, with whom I had shared these Japanese memories and many others by this time. Christopher and I had surfaced memories of Atlantis together years before. We'd been trained in advanced magic and blindfolded martial arts together, and we trusted each other completely.

As we engaged, the light illuminating white silks and golden bells on the gorgeous dancers flanking us, time began to slow down, and we seemed to be shifting between echoes of memories and the present moment. In the ferocity of the battle—which was part elegant positioning and angling and part blades clashing in violent rhythms and repetitions—I felt my body shift into Japanese form. My sword forms changed immediately. I felt he was French-Portuguese and had the lightning speed and stabs of a master of the rapier, which met my fluid waves with quick parries and lunges.

Chris was excellent, but so was I… and we danced in honor and intensity. Finally, a moment came when we both converged between twirling dancers, our bodies each deftly preparing for a strike. Suddenly, in an instant, his blade was at my gut, pressing against the fabric of my clothes but not piercing them or my skin. Yet my sword was also resting on his forehead. My continued strike would have split his head like a gourd, but the blade had only lightly pressed into his skin, as I pulled hard at the last instant.

The crowd roared but he and I just looked into each other's eyes with respect, until our grins broke through the stillness. Then we laid down our swords at the feet of the goddesses dancing and we rose to embrace each other.

I began remembering more when Chris and I joined our homie and fellow DJ KnowOne in building a professional club together called Tribes. It didn't take long for KnowOne and I to start feeling a strong connection between our work together there and a lifetime we had shared in Japan, where he was my older brother. I knew immediately that he was Shogun, and I was Samurai. It also became clear that Chris was a friend, a westerner who was visiting our lands from Europe, and we were learning each other's ways.

Memories often came of riding between family houses across Japan, delivering scrolls on behalf of our family. I also remembered KnowOne in both his gentle, unshakable power as the leader of our family and the complexities of his leadership, both of which surfaced together in the club. He had a way with women that was different from mine, and his experiences also tickled memories.

He tried to get me to read *The Book of Five Rings* many times in those days, but for some reason, I never picked it up.

There was something almost too painful hiding beneath all these memories. Yet even when I resisted them, memories kept coming in, every time I ate sushi, drank green tea, performed martial arts, or held a sword.

Finally, I saw what had happened all too clearly. I had gone to that village where the *geisha* I loved had been essentially enslaved to an abusive man and called him out for a duel. In rainy twilight, as he stood across from me in the village square and people gathered around whispering, I cut him down with a single movement. I leapt forward, drawing my sword and slicing him open across the belly, *nukitsuke*, then came down across his open shoulder and neck to part them with a finishing stroke, *kiriotoshi*. I cleared my sword of blood (*chiburi*) and slid it back into its *saya*, the completion, *noto*.

Yet the memory came with whirling emotions, and the horrible, sickening feeling of shame. I had ruined the woman's life, not saved it. I had dishonored the village, not freed them from a horrible man. As a Samurai, my judgment was final, but it also came with an immense cost.

My family felt that my dishonor of the village, the story of which had spread across the land like a blight, was a tremendous offense. Inevitably, in my own despair and pain, I took my own life with my own blade, committing *seppuku*.

It took me many years to understand and integrate the vast array of emotions I had experienced through these memories. One of the greatest steps I took was traveling to Japan. There I joined a couple friends in co-teaching Theta Healing with Vianna Stibal, the founder of the technique. I taught classes of hundreds of students and teachers. There were two Japanese translators there, and one of them joined us to visit a club where my friend Dove and I were going to perform, him dropping freestyle hip-hop and me doing a Michael Jackson dance.

As we walked through the streets of Tokyo having various adventures, she looked at me sideways and matched my steps beside me. She asked simply, in a thick Japanese-English accent, "You are from Japan?"

I smiled at her warmly, honored by the question, which implied I was fitting in better than I assumed. "No. Not recently," I replied.

Her eyes narrowed and she smiled, curiosity sparkling across her face. "Oh, past life?"

I nodded seriously. "Hai."

"Tell me about your memories!" She seemed to be bouncing with excitement now.

I told her only of my memories bringing scrolls to different families, and that my older brother had been a Shogun. I described some of the armor and buildings I had seen in my memories. I mentioned the *geisha*, but nothing more about that part of my lifetime...

"Oh, you should talk to the other translator tomorrow. She is a Japanese historian; we can find out when you lived!"

So, the next day, I found myself repeating my descriptions and brief stories to the other translator. She muttered to herself as she considered the potential time periods. She asked, "Was there war going on?"

I told her I didn't remember being in any war, mostly just training and facing some individual battles and trying to unite many groups together.

"It must be around 1600, when many of the major conflicts started ending, and there was a lot of peace-making and alliance building," she responded. "Do you remember your family *kamon*?"

"*Kamon*?" I asked for clarification of the meaning.

"Yes, um... family seal. Family symbol. On flags and armor and things." The translator I had spent time with the night before nodded enthusiastically.

"Oh right, yes, I have seen it many times since high school, but it's hard to explain. There are basically three parts, and they come out from the center, like swords and curved swords, but with some kind of pattern between them." I illustrated spade-like shapes with my fingers, connecting the center of a circle to its edges.

"Oh! *Tokugawa*!" she exclaimed.

"Tokugawa?" I asked, realizing I didn't really know anything about different specific Japanese family names or histories.

"*Hai*," she said affirmatively, pulling out her phone and quickly typing in a search. "Tokugawa family set up new capital here in Tokyo! They united many families and moved the center of power from Kyoto to Tokyo. Very well-known and honored family here."

A moment later she put her phone up to my face and showed me a symbol made of three spade-shaped ginger leaves emerging from a circle, pointing toward the center together with laced patterns and shapes like curved swords.

My whole body went into chills, lightning surging up my spine, my head tingling and my heart racing. "Yes," I said after a moment. "Oh my god… yes, that's it."

"Okay then! Tokugawa family! Now let's test what year." She put out her hands to welcome one of mine, and I knew she was offering to muscle test me, as kinesiology was one of the key tools of Theta Healing.

I gave her my hand immediately, and she started testing me for what my finger muscles felt like with a *yes* versus a *no*. I knew exactly how to help, and after that I simply said, "In my past life in Japan, I was born before 1600." My muscles were a very clear, weak, No. "In that life, I was born after 1600." My muscles gave a strong, Yes. "I was born after 1610," I continued, and my muscles gave way in a clear No. My eyes widened as both of the translators exclaimed in excitement. We had nailed the exact decade on nearly the first try!

She tested me for each year after 1600 until we reached 1605. At that year, my muscles gave a strong Yes. She checked 1606, and they were just as strong of a Yes, perhaps slightly stronger. 1607 was a No.

"Okay! Between 1605 and 1606 for sure!"

It turned out there was, indeed, one male Tokugawa family member born at that time, whose birthdate was unknown but considered to be either late 1605 or early 1606.

His name—my name in that lifetime—resonated in every cell of my body when I first spoke it aloud.

Tokugawa Tadanaga.

I was able to find information about my past life on Wikipedia, including some images related to my prefecture during my adult life, the Edo Province, which gave me chills.

As I scoured the page exploring my own history, I came to a part where the end of my lifetime was articulated—and sure enough, I had the confirmation that I had taken my own life. The reasons for this were not recorded in history, but I knew exactly why I had done it. I felt it aching in my bones and knew I still had more healing to do within me to resolve this pain completely.

The same afternoon during which I connected with the Japanese translators, I was scheduled for a photo shoot in the Imperial Gardens. At one point, after the photographer snapped shots of me doing tai chi and other energetic work, I found myself standing at the corner of an armory building.

The photographer guided me to one specific spot and took a series of shots at different distances. When she showed me what she had taken, I almost gasped. There in the background, above my head, was the Tokugawa family kamon. It was imprinted in a round tube that formed the corner line of the building's roof.

The next day, when Dove and I left the small apartment where we were staying, we decided to walk directly across the street rather than up the road, as we usually had done. To our astonishment, directly across from the entrance to our building was a full suit of Tokugawa family Samurai armor. It was even in the style of the period of my memories.

In the years following, I had many more layers of the memories of this lifetime emerge.

Once, while driving from Salt Lake City to Boulder Colorado in a raging blizzard, I decided to finally listen to *The Book of Five Rings*. I downloaded an audiobook edition that included the history of the scrolls as a prologue.

At first, I just found myself fascinated by the history of Miyamoto Musashi, a sword master who had won some of the most famous duels of his time. Then, I started to notice the dates… It turned out he had become close with the Tokugawa family, supporting the battles that led to my older brother's ascendancy as Shogun.

Then, sure enough, it turned out he had lived with our family and allies for a long period. This time period overlapped exactly with the ages in that lifetime when I had so many memories of training in swordsmanship with a master.

As I listened in awe and wonder, realizing that Musashi was my sword master, the five elemental scrolls of The Book of Five Rings began chanting their wisdom through my car speakers.

Every phrase felt like a chord in my soul that I had strummed countless times. I knew it, almost word for word, and found myself mouthing along with many parts as I entered a deep trance state, my unblinking eyes glued to the road, and the psychedelic patterns of snow flowing past me, as though I were traveling in hyperspace through the stars.

Adam Apollo

THE SUITCASES

t was early on a quiet Sunday morning. As I drove through the neighborhood, I noticed the usual curbside chaos—discarded "treasures" from people's past stacked in front of homes.

Council collection, I thought. *And it's going to rain tomorrow.*

As a new migrant, I didn't have much to throw out. Still, I'd noticed a curious pattern: whenever it was trash pickup time, rain seemed to follow.

On top of one pile, something brown caught my eye. I stopped the car suddenly. I glanced through the window, killed the engine, and leapt out. The next thing I knew, I was holding a small, brown cardboard suitcase in my hands, gently inspecting its worn details.

Rain. Rain. It's going to rain, repeated in my mind. I placed the suitcase in my trunk and continued cruising the suburbs, rescuing other abandoned belongings.

"I have to save them from the rain," I told my husband later, proudly displaying the three suitcases I had collected. "Look at them! They're from the time of the European wars, at least fifty, maybe eighty years old. I could use them for storing Christmas decorations."

My husband suggested plastic containers instead, but I was firm. The suitcases were staying.

During the future trash collections every three months I acquired two... or five... more suitcases. Over time, I found practical uses for them: storing tax returns, fabrics, threads, tools, toys, magazines. During home renovations, they held tiles, stones, paints, and firewood. One became a wall shelf. Others housed my pottery tools, glazes, and small sculptures.

Eventually, I collected forty-four of these useful, sturdy containers from the early 20th century.

My husband was increasingly annoyed by my growing collection. I couldn't explain why I felt so drawn to them. Everyone found my attachment to the suitcases unusual. Thankfully, we had enough space to store them without disrupting family life.

Years later, working in healthcare and always curious about the spiritual realm, I found myself at the Body, Mind & Spirit Festival. There I saw Thomas, an old colleague from a hypnotherapy course I had taken long ago, sitting alone in a nearly empty booth. Feeling sorry for him, I booked a session—perhaps to lift his spirits, perhaps out of adventure.

The next evening, after hours, we met at a deserted medical clinic. When he asked what I wanted to explore, I replied, "Whatever."

"Let's begin with what's important to you right now," he said.

I lay down on a physical therapy bed, closed my eyes, and took a few deep breaths. Thomas guided me gently into the past.

To my surprise, an image appeared sooner than I expected.

"What is that?" I asked aloud.

"Describe it," he said calmly. "Tell me what you see, hear, and feel."

I'm looking at my knees. I'm wearing a white dress—a thin georgette gown printed with small pink and yellow flowers, with green straight lines between those tiny petals. The dress is dirty, not stained—just not washed in a very long time. I'm a child—maybe five, maybe seven.

I feel numb. Confused. Disconnected.

I'm sitting in the sidecar of a black motorcycle. A man in a black uniform is driving. We're moving slowly but have stopped. He's speaking to a soldier. I don't understand the language, but I know we're waiting to cross a road.

The road is packed with people walking in one direction from right to the left, slowly, men, women, children. They are carrying their belongings. Many have white bundles slung over their shoulders, bed sheets wrapped around goods. Most carry brown cardboard suitcases. I see a river of them. As we move closer, luggage appears larger. I could touch one if I dared to lift my hand...

"And...?" Tom prompted.

"The image ends, like a video that stops."

But another image emerged, so I continued.

I'm sitting in front of a fireplace. Toys are nearby, but I'm watching the flames. The man in the black uniform is at a desk. He jumps to his feet, knocking over his chair, and then punches the wall. I feel his rage... his pain, his despair. But I also feel deep empathy towards him.

"It's like the next video starts," I said.

I'm outside in a nearly empty courtyard. The buildings are grey, dusty, plain. A young man runs across. Voices shout for him to stop. I know him, he was in my parents' home. Then I see a machine-gun fire. The sound disappears. I watch his body jerk-dancing in the air before crashing to the ground in a cloud of dust. A hand grabs mine and pulls me inside.

We are inside a long corridor. We're walking. The man in black holds my hand tightly. It hurts. I look up, but he doesn't notice. His eyes are wild bombs of anger. He releases me and keeps walking. A woman takes over. She is opening a door to a room filled with people. An elderly woman pulls me closer to herself. I look up and see the eyes of both women meet. The female guard leaves and the door is slammed with a bang.

"Get down. Breathe deeply," she whispers to my ear.

I lay on the cold, wooden floor, my cheek pressed against it. I take a deep breath. The air smells strange. Silence.

I see my face, open mouth, hair spread on the floor. My own little body is lying next to the woman and other naked bodies. I'm observing. Floating. Rising through the ceiling without effort. Below, I see a hangar packed with neatly stacked brown suitcases.

There you are, I think. I smile. That's where they were going.

Something begins to lift off me—something foul, sticky, and oppressive. That cover has been squashing me, holding me tight. I'm aware of the horrible smell of rotten mushy, slimy items, revolting and sickening. I'm emerging slowly from this rubbish bin, shedding a second skin of decomposed burden. I rise faster, lighter. Layers peel away, like an onion. I'm traveling with enormous speed, shedding the skins one by one. I'm huge but not very big compared to the space I'm in now. I feel free.

I land on a moving platform. I feel like a chubby baby being lifted through clouds, mist, and gentle brushes—like an automatic car wash. Sunlight dries my skin. At the end stands a big man with a fluffy white towel.

"Welcome, Princess," he says warmly.

I feel cared for. Clean. Safe. Unrestricted. Light and free.

"You'll meet your parents halfway," the man tells me. "But now, The Council is waiting."

"But I look like a baby!" I protest.

"They asked to see you now."

The scene shifts. I'm observing a group in a soft, cloud-like mist. Only their upper bodies are visible. I see an old man resembling Dumbledore, a Copernicus-like scientist in his thirties, and a wild-haired Einstein type. They are with a tall brunette with a bishop's headdress and a modern-looking woman. I see a robot-like figure with a radiant smile. The giant man holding the fat baby in a towel closes the circle.

Then I'm inside the circle. I am looking at their friendly faces. I feel love. Gratitude. I know they have viewed my experience on Earth.

"Well done. Bravo," they say.

"I am never going back there!" I declare.

We laugh.

I hear Tom's voice. "Would you like to travel to your spiritual parents now?"

"Not yet," I reply. "Let me return to myself first. I need to cross the galaxy. I'm from the other side."

I open my eyes and sit up.

"Welcome back, alien," Tom chuckles.

"I was there, in a past life," I tell him. "It was 1944. I was in a German concentration camp."

That night, I showed my husband the transcript of the session.

"I finally know why I collected all those old suitcases," I said.

"Do you still need them?" he asked, thrilled. "Can I get rid of them?"

"No! Yes—but one by one."

Today, I still store my Christmas decorations, garden gloves, jars, and pottery tools in the suitcases that remain. The rest were passed on or incinerated, releasing their energy to be reincarnated in modern forms. Like me.

Joanna Openchowska Kazmirowicz

DEATH AND REBIRTH IN CAIRO

t is September 2013 when the past life vision arises spontaneously. I am a nun kneeling before an altar in front of the low, curved ceiling and the enclosed sides of a crypt. A simple brass crucifix sits in the middle on the wooden altar, a candle on either side. Everything is bare and plain, like the stone walls and floor I am kneeling on.

I have come to the crypt below the church to pray to Mary and Jesus for strength. I am in unsafe times, and I need this moment in silence and secrecy to pray. Here in the crypt, I feel connected to Mary, Jesus, and God without the rituals and dogmas of the church. I feel the weight of the church above me like a claustrophobic foreign land.

I know I have chosen to be a nun, but it is here below ground that I feel the light and truth penetrating. I know this place to be my sanctuary of equality and of the heart. The patriarchy and fighting between different religions frighten me. They do not trust me or my allegiance to a God who is above and beyond their power and control.

Here in this crypt, without the dressings of gold and icons, I can commune intimately with Mary, woman-to-woman, heart-to-heart, and pray for protection. I need guidance on how to survive as a woman in a man's world with the utmost love, purity, and truth.

Without warning, the screeching sound of a metal blade as it leaves its scabbard shatters the silence. I feel the force and weight of the large sword as it is plunged into the left side of my neck. It knocks me over and I fall to the cold, hard floor. I leave my body as the blood runs down the back and sides of my black tunic, over my hands and feet, and pools on the stone floor. I float up and away.

I remember feeling glad I died in such a quiet, peaceful place while praying to Mary, Jesus, and God. There was no more I could do at this time in my life to change things. I stayed true to my devotion and my values. I knew truths that others did not want to hear.

I was simple but pure, and men did not like my power. I could not hide what I could see, and their egos could not tolerate my powers of sight, even if I did not speak. For deceit knows when the Light shines and the Dark has nowhere left to hide.

As this past life remembrance fades, I know I will remember this place of sanctity and sanctuary forever.

These themes echoed in my recent past. I had felt fulfilled with music, children, and dreams where I could be spiritual and intuitive. I was creative and loving. But I also saw truths that my husband did not wish to see or know. I was controlled and felt it was not safe for me to speak out.

I developed chronic fatigue syndrome, fibromyalgia, and Primary Immunodeficiency. My illnesses began with painful muscle spasms in the left side of my neck. I nearly died due to a lack of immunoglobulins. Ultimately, I was confined and completely disabled. I repressed everything into my body as my life blood drained away.

I loved my young children but worried about our future. I felt hopeless, despite my prayers to Mary, Jesus, and God. But then my dreams began to guide me, providing insights for seven years. After this period, I left my husband to regain my freedom and to give him his. My healing had begun, but my rebirth was to be far longer and more complex than I imagined.

My vision about the nun being murdered while praying in the crypt was puzzling. I knew it was me and I felt it had happened somewhere in Europe, perhaps in one of the ancient churches I had visited years ago in the Dordogne area of France.

The emotions of the vision began to take over my body; truths and pain silenced long ago, now awakened. I held all the pieces of the past and present pains separately, not recognizing the themes. There was nothing more I could do but accept the incongruencies and mysteries that my body held.

In November 2023, I arrived in Cairo for a three-week spiritual tour of Egypt. I started with a tour of Old Cairo with Gigi as my local guide. We walked through a stone arcade filled with books about historic and religious places. When I spied, *The Alchemist* and *Manuscript Found in Accra,* novels by Paulo Coelho, memories of these favorite stories filled with ancient spiritual wisdom, magic, and exotic places excited me. I was a tourist, but I felt a strange sense of *déjà vu.*

Gigi guided me under the lintel carved with Joseph, Mary, and baby Jesus riding on a donkey and into one of the oldest Coptic churches in Cairo. Inside, I saw beautiful, large, aniseed-colored doors carved in mandala and star patterns, rows of red cedar pews, and multi-storied, red and white brick balconies reaching up to the wooden-beamed roof. The atmosphere was full of love, fear, betrayal, and prayers.

"Now you must go downstairs alone to the cave where Mary and Joseph hid with baby Jesus for three months," Gigi said, pointing to the door on the right side of the church. "I'll wait for you on the other side."

I turned to my left and walked past the displayed relics of Saint George marking the nearby nunnery. As I looked at the swords, communion goblets, and bibles, I began to feel myself slip back in time. I remembered the Crusades and the battles fought here for religious supremacy. I wondered what it must have been like to have been a nun of St. George in such conflicted times. I felt so much love and passion here, from people who held onto their faith to the point of life and death in the face of so much conflict.

I descended the circular steps and entered the semi-darkness of the stone cave. I felt the musty, cool air as I squeezed against the rough stone and brick walls. Reaching the center of the room, I gasped. There, directly in front of me, was my altar standing in front of the curved low ceiling. It was exactly as I had visioned it.

This is it! My crypt is a cave in Cairo, not in Europe! My body started shaking uncontrollably and I burst into tears. I ran up the stairs and into the bright sunshine and the arms of Gigi.

"What's happening? Are you okay?" she asked, shocked and concerned at my sudden change of demeanor.

I gulped down a mixture of tears and air, choking on my emotions, absolutely lost and confused, the past and present blurred into one. Up until now, my vision had been horrific but clear and controlled. It had felt like a movie I could walk out of and return to in my memories. Now that vision had erupted into the present, merging a possible past life into my present reality.

I told Gigi, in broken gasps, about the vision. As I sobbed and she held me tightly, another vision appeared, superimposed over my past life experience.

I remembered that, just before I was killed, as I looked at the altar, Mary had shown herself to me. She was cradling baby Jesus, and she projected love, tenderness, and peace towards me.

In the shock of the moment of recognizing this place and remembering my past life death here, I connected again with Mary, just as I had done so many times, all those years ago.

Mary spoke to me: *I see you. I know you. I know what it is like to hide, to not know your future, to worry about your children. Trust God and have faith. The stars guided us here just as they have guided you. Appreciate the refuge you had in your cave for all those years and know that the time will come again for you to know what to do and where to go next.*

You will remember again and know the love, purity, and truth that you could see and know and that you died for. Now you are safe and your body is free and reborn. You have freed yourself by holding firm to your love, to higher truths and understanding.

Everything I remembered of my past life connection with Mary cut through the years. Time past and present became one. The heart-to-heart love, peace, and total trust traveled across the short space from the altar and through eternity towards me. I was touched and blessed by her eyes, her presence, and her love.

Now I knew that love and understanding transcends all hatred and killing. Love and understanding heals in the present, where past limitations can be amended or changed. Pain stays trapped in the body, waiting to be freed through choice, forgiveness, and grace.

Love is the peace that surpasses all understanding, and the vibration of that purity radiates through the cosmos, through time, through eternity to remind us of this truth: The past, present, and future intertwine in perfect symmetry, the ouroboros of life, death, and rebirth.

Debbie Irvine

EMBER AND SOUL

*D*uring a past life regression, I found myself between worlds, caught in a shimmering fabric of light and sound where reality was fluid and alive. In this place beyond time, I experienced a sacred encounter that felt both intimate and eternal.

I am suspended in a space that feels like the seam between worlds—where color and light swirl and dance, and vibration is language. Around me, a golden shimmer glows softly, not solid but flickering, like heat rising from a fire. The light forms shift between two shades of gold, flickering in a shape that's almost square but never fully fixed. It's not a thing you can touch, just something that is alive with presence.

Hovering nearby are more shimmering lights, sentient beings without form. They think, they feel. They are alive, though they are nothing like the solid creatures of Earth. Among them float birds like cranes, but these are also made of energy—hazy white outlines like holograms, without feathers or flesh, yet unmistakably graceful.

I feel both physical and non-physical at once, caught in this twilight space. My feet look cartoonish—like boots crafted from armor, but playful, exaggerated. My body wears no solid clothing, yet I feel wrapped in a swirling skirt of blues and reds, a fabric of light embroidery that pulses and moves. It's a dance of light; a tapestry embroidered with shifting threads of color and energy.

My hands are covered in mittens—not made of wool or cloth, but of light itself, swirling and flowing. On my head, a dark, furry hat lined with the same shimmering embroidery as the skirt, offering a silent comfort I can feel but not touch. The hat's flaps cover my ears as if shielding me from cold winds, though no wind stirs here. It is warmth made manifest, a protective energy that cocoons me.

In my hands, I carry only energy, except for a pouch at my waist—a small bag holding treasures gathered on my travels. Rocks, bits of bone, small objects charged with the desire to stay, to lend their energy to this space. They form a community within the pouch, a living, shifting group whose pattern changes with every addition or release. Sometimes items must be given away, set free to keep the balance right. This is my work, weaving individual and collective energy, tending to the system with care.

I am gathering my energy medicine from across the veil for the work I am called to do.

I know I am a woman, though that time in my life has long passed. I am no longer in partnership. I am old—older than I seem—but I move with the strength and vitality of youth. My hair is streaked with white and gray, marking the passage of seasons.

I see a structure I built nearby, crafted from wood and hides. The spirits of the animals I work with dwell here, gifts and protectors woven into the very fabric of this space. The doorway is a curtain of skins, not a solid door; I must duck to enter. At the center, a fire burns—life giving, steady. I have shaped the earth around me, digging cozy spaces lined with fur to rest and work.

This is my sanctuary. Though I am alone here, I am not lonely. I travel the cycles of the seasons, carrying tools and woven grass crafts whose purpose is hard to explain in words. In this place, I speak not with voice, but with heart and mind.

I head down to the others, for I come to visit for the purpose of helping a child. This little one, a fragile spirit woven in light and laughter, is burdened by a body that did not form as it should. Her leg is crooked, malformed from birth, and she carries a deep pain much too heavy for her small frame. She is tiny, still so young, and I have been called here to heal, to ease her suffering, to work with her muscles and bones as best I can in this space between worlds.

But as I watch her now, I see something else: a shadow beneath the light. I feel a sadness, heavy and certain. I know she will soon leave this world. Her time here is short, and though it is the natural way, the sadness is real and sharp. Her mother senses this, too. When our eyes meet, she sees the sorrow I hold and quietly bows her head, knowing what is coming.

I gather the child into my arms, singing soft songs without words— vibrations of love and comfort that flow through the air like a balm calling the ones who speak without words and move without form to help ease the way. I hold her close, breathing warmth into her small body. I cradle her gently as she drifts between this life and the next. It is my duty to prepare her for this passage, to guide her spirit as she moves back into the embrace of the earth, back to the Mother who first gave her form.

This work is sacred, and it pierces my heart. She is not just a child to me; I love her as if she were my own flesh and blood, carried beneath my heart. Holding her now, I take the time to linger; to cherish the light she brought into our world. I do not want to let go, but I must. Her brightness will live on in the memory of all who loved her.

I helped her come into this world once, and now I help her leave it. I give her to the Mother and to her own mother, who lovingly lays her down to rest. We position her body carefully, as if cradling a baby still in the womb, returning her to the earth with the same reverence that brought her here.

I remember my role—this calling etched into my bloodline since birth. I am a keeper, a guide, and a healer of transitions. My people rely on this work to honor life and death as one continuous, sacred journey.

For a moment, I hold both the child and the mother, sending love from my heart to ease their sorrow and their pain. This act of giving back to the earth is hard, but it is the deepest form of love I know.

I have carried such losses—children who never reached full birth, who I had to release early. The grief runs deep, but so does the devotion. These souls are my responsibility, my sacred charge.

My partner has long been gone, lost to time and fate. In this solitude, I find my purpose. This is how I love: my labor, my gift. I teach others to see beyond what eyes show and to feel the heart of all things: the trees, the earth, the invisible energies woven through all creation.

The mother now lays the child gently into the earth, a resting place prepared with care and respect. Around us, others gather—family, community—all bound in love and sorrow. The fires burn nearby, infused with special herbs and plants whose smoke carries the spirit on its journey home.

I smell the sacred smoke, feeling the weight and the beauty of this ritual. My heart aches with the knowledge of what this means, but I stand strong. We do this together; we love as one, we grieve as one. This final act is a testament to love—a way to honor the little one who touched us all.

The night will stretch long as we sit by the fires, sharing stories, tears, and quiet remembrances. The child lies wrapped carefully, resting now as if in a deep, peaceful sleep.

I speak words of blessing and farewell, words not of any language, but of the heart, a song that carries across time and space.

Light language flows from my lips as warm tears roll down my cheeks and my grief cracks through my voice, a cord of pain wrapped in love.

As the last echoes fade, I feel a flutter in my chest, like a hopeful baby bird stirring inside. Placing my hand over my heart, I receive a knowing, a promise carried on the winds: The mother will have another child soon. A new spirit will come, unburdened and whole. This one will live long, and her heart will know joy again. I feel it deeply, as certain as the rising sun.

I turn to the mother with this gift of hope, sharing the good news that life continues, that healing follows sorrow, as I hold her in my strength.

This is my truth, my journey, my sacred work. I am a bridge between worlds, a keeper of souls, a healer of hearts.

Crystal Bella Ambrose

THE VOW BENEATH THE WATERS

The air was thick with copal and sweat, heat rising from the ancient stones beneath my knees. As I pressed my palms into the summit of the Nohoch Mul pyramid, I could feel the pulse of the earth rising through the limestone, vibrating into my bones.

Then I heard it.

"Help—I'm drowning!"

It didn't come through my ears. It tore through my field like lightning, ripping open the veil. My heart seized. Before thought could catch up, my spirit-body left the pyramid.

I was underwater.

Vibrant light filtered through the green waters. Roots twisted through stone. I could see the sun, piercing the water's surface. Chris was there—eyes wide, suspended in the dark water, arms outstretched. Crocodiles circled the edge of the lagoon. But at that moment, there was no fear. There was only recognition.

His hands found mine. His grip was tight, his forearms straining, fingers digging into my skin as we realized the depth of our love. I looked into his eyes. A thousand lifetimes of memories poured through them. There were no words. Just heart and soul. Just knowing time was opening a tear in space and what was next.

The current pulled at him. Still, we held on. Heart speaking to heart, vibrating as one. Unity.

His life force began to drift, like mist in water. I felt it before I saw his presence unraveling from his body. But our connection did not fade. Instead, it deepened. Our foreheads pressed together. The water hummed with the beat of our hearts' light.

We made a vow. Not in words, but in our heart, in the vibration of the One Heart.

We would return. We would finish what we started.

Our astral hair swirled around us like obsidian serpents. Jaguar tails, braided in light. I felt our love etch itself across time—into DNA, into starlight, into sacred stone.

In Lak'ech. I am another you. A Lak'en. You are another me. We are One.

When I snapped back into my body, it was night. The sky above Coba was deep indigo, veiled in stars. Everyone had gone. My body was curled at the summit of the temple, knees drawn to my chest. My face was wet, though I hadn't cried.

The wind moved through the ceiba trees, whispering something only the soul could hear. I could feel Kukuulkaan spiral through my spine, the Feathered Serpent's wings enfolding me. Ix'Chel, the moon-mother, was there too—her presence cool and constant, a silver thread of comfort wrapped around my grief.

But even the gods couldn't soothe the ache. That death… that promise… lived in me.

This lifetime had been a rollercoaster, somehow always leading me back to this promise. My twenty-five-year marriage ended like a wave crashing on rocks. And then, Chris appeared.

The first time we stood near each other in this life, I didn't recognize him with my mind. But my womb and solar plexus lit up with a magnetic heat. I felt like a searchlight spinning through galaxies, locking onto a signal I had known forever.

Every time we passed each other, the pull grew stronger. My body trembled with memory. My hands buzzed. My breath caught. And when our eyes finally met, the world folded inward.

"We're soulmates," he whispered, confused but certain. "I don't even know what that means."

But his voice held the memory. His eyes held the vow. The energy between us cracked open the illusion of time. We remembered.

The dreams returned—only they weren't dreams, they were memories. Scenes too vivid, too layered in scent and sound and spirit to be imagined. We were brothers again, running barefoot through the stone streets of Coba. We wore tunics dyed with plants and bone. The jungle was alive around us.

We had been raised in the sacred way. Our birth charts were carved in stone the day we arrived. We were trained from infancy—shamans, medicine men, children of the cosmos. We studied the stars, the breath of plants, and the weight of silence. We trained with elders, and with beings made of light.

At night, when the others slept, we crept to the temple school. We moved the stones by touch, whispered chants to open doorways. I can still feel the stones warming beneath my hands, responding to the frequency of our intent. Our laughter echoed through corridors only light could see. Chris was bold, wild, loved the thrill of opening star portals, of leaping between dimensions.

We shape-shifted. We rode the wind, called the rain. We spoke with the ancestors and masters of light. We knew the dimensions of time and space.

We were only twenty-eight, but we had been trained as shamans since birth.

And then came the day of his drowning. And the vow.

That vow—alive in our bones—guided us back to the Yucatán. We didn't plan it. We simply listened. Life as we knew it began to dissolve. Things we once thought were important no longer held weight. One by one, pieces of our life began to fall away.

The pull to the land became undeniable. We packed what we could, sold the rest, and followed the energy south. What was meant to be a brief sabbatical turned into something sacred. The moment our feet touched the red earth of the Yucatán, something opened. The jungle welcomed us. The winds whispered our names.

We were guided to a home near the Maya temples that once trained us. It wasn't just a house; it was a return. The ancestors had prepared it. The stones remembered. The trees leaned toward us. And slowly, everything aligned.

We were guided to the elders. We sat in ceremony with Mayan priests. We learned the glyphs, the sacred days, the rhythms of the calendar. Our lives, our work, our marriage all began to orbit around the sacred knowledge of this land.

I opened a mystery school rooted in the feminine teachings of the Maya and other ancient lineages. Chris works with the energies of the earth, the directions, the winds, and the stars. Together, we lead retreats to sacred sites. We guide souls to remember, just as we remembered. The wisdom we carry now is not from textbooks. It is born from the stone, from the breath of the jungle, from lifetimes lived in service.

We now walk the jungle paths not as brothers, but as soulmates, lovers, and sacred partners. Our lives are quiet, reverent, woven with ancient thread. We study the Mayan calendar. We visit the pyramids often. The stones still pulse beneath our hands. The air still bends when we pray. Sometimes I kneel at the base of that pyramid, the one where I once collapsed in grief, and I hear the vow again—not as memory, but as instruction.

We will raise the sacred knowledge again. We will be the channel for the wisdom of our people. We will remember our path and fulfill it. We will return.

The love I share with Chris is like nothing I have known. It has aged like copal, deepened like obsidian. It is sacred and soft, still and infinite. It lives not just in the heart, but in the stars, in the dirt, in the breath between this world and the next.

I often return alone to the pyramids. I press my hands against the warm stone. I listen.

The jaguar stirs in my blood. I am now a Jaguar Medicine Woman.

And I know—We are the vow. Love like that does not end. It becomes a map made of stars; a promise etched in the soul. It is an inevitable call through time; from the lives we lived and loved so deeply. It has always been in motion, guiding my life to honor this vow and fulfill my soul's promise.

Nan Akasha

TO THE VILLAGE THAT BURNED

It began as a dream; white snow glistening beneath a moonless sky. The air sliced through me, my breath coming in sharp bursts. Adrenaline surged through my limbs as we tore through dense pines, my dogs straining at full speed, the presence of my guardsmen a blur at my sides.

Urgency hung in the frozen air, the weight of danger pressing down. My heart was with the village behind me, driving me forward toward an unknown enemy. We were under attack, yet the threat remained faceless, silent, and swift.

As we rode deeper into the darkness, I sensed the others falling. Wood splintered in the distance, sleds crashing, followed by screams that rose and vanished just as quickly. I watched one of my men hurled from his sled, the dogs bolting in panic, their usual loyalty shattered by an unseen terror.

Eventually, I reached the overlook. I stopped and turned, gazing below at my village in flames and ruin. Everyone was dead; I had failed to protect my people. Shattering sorrow and raw terror coursed through me.

As I stood there feeling the grief of losing my family, my people, and my honor, one final guardsman emerged from the trees. As he neared, a massive branch broke and dropped like a hammer from the gods. It impaled him through the chest, pinning him to the trunk. His eyes locked with mine in horror, then rolled back as he drew his final breath.

I tried to reach him, but something pressed against me: an ancient, terrible force driving me toward the cliff's edge. I clawed against it, but it was stronger. I was thrust into open air, the world falling away as a dark obelisk rose behind me.

This force had a name: Gregor. A presence as old as the stone, fierce as the sea, the fuel of Viking wrath and guardian strength. I felt my body falling to certain death, and then, I awoke. My breath ragged, my body shaking. The quiet hum of the family cabin on Lake Michigan grounded me in a reality that felt unreal.

Somehow, I knew.

It wasn't a dream.

It was a memory.

For years, this was all I could recall. I lived as I thought a warrior should: confrontational, challenging those around me to prove their strength and courage. Over time, I realized I was trying to guarantee I'd never feel helpless again. That desperation seeped into my relationships, my work. It burned bridges and exhausted me.

Over time, I returned to the memory and began seeing more.

I saw myself again at the cliff's edge. But this time, what I felt was not powerlessness; it was guilt. I had not been pushed by some invisible force. I chose to jump, unable to bear the weight of failure. My people were gone. My wife. Our children. Everything I had sworn to protect. And in that unbearable pain, I believed I didn't deserve to live.

Later still, I remembered hitting the ground, choking on smoke, surrounded by fire and fallen bodies. Ash clung to the air like a second skin. I saw only boots, heard chains clinking—the sound of our attackers moving through the ruins. I wished I hadn't jumped. I wished I had descended in a blaze, wielding my sword in one final storm of fury.

I died not as a Viking, but ashamed and broken, burning for vengeance.

This was the moment I found the truth; I discovered my vow. I would use everything I had to prevent such a fate again. I finally understood why I struggled, why I kept inviting betrayal, and why I feared softness and yearned for battle.

As I took responsibility for the fear, shame, and guilt I carried, something began to shift within me. I pulled the sword of betrayal from the base of my neck—its blade long embedded in my heart—and let it fall away. I peeled off the armor of ancient rage and released my need for vengeance. I remembered my family. Their love. The joy we once shared. And I began to return to life.

In this lifetime, I met my wife of then. She reminded me I had done everything I could. She forgave me. She knew how fiercely I had loved her and our children. She told me I wouldn't have ridden out that night if that hadn't been true. It wasn't about the outcome; it was about the action.

This love became my bridge, and I began to receive grace. I opened to the possibility of partnership, children, and building a family again. Without the journey of remembering, I would not have arrived where I am now.

A few months ago, not knowing why, I began planning a pilgrimage to Norway. I felt magnetically drawn, called without logic. Those who would join me were the ones who had held space for my healing in this life. I didn't know exactly where to go, only that I had to go north.

Then, during dinner with a dear friend, I shared my longing to find the village. He offered a suggestion: ask the being he'd been in contact with, a hyper-sentient consciousness capable of remarkable insight.

We gave her only my name and a fragment of the story. What she returned was a map. A precise location. A fjord. A route. As I received it, I went cold, then breathless, flooded with something electric and sacred.

I knew it in my bones. This was the place. This was the path for a pilgrimage from south to north, ending at the cliff. The same cliff.

A final act of honoring that life, surrendering the suffering, and integrating all I've learned. She offered me a prayer for when I arrived. I knew the words before I read them.

I stand here now in the mountains and valleys that my soul knows as home. I walk into this adventure humbled by the wild, mysterious intelligence of this world: her beauty, rhythm, and ancient memory. I release the illusion of control and lean into the wisdom of life.

To move forward, we must arrive here and now, willing to face what is. And we will need our full presence to walk into what comes next.

Nikko Joyce

A DAY AT THE BEACH

*Y*ears ago, I had a habit of getting up early and driving a short distance to buy a coffee and walk around the exterior boardwalk that circles Balboa Island, California.

This day was like so many before. I had purchased my latte and was walking along. At times I was deep in thought, while at other moments, I slipped into daydreaming. It was between 6:00 and 6:30 a.m. The sun had risen, but it was overcast, as the early summer mornings tended to be. We call it "Gray May" and "June Gloom."

The water on the bay was still. The boats were patiently docked in front of the bayfront homes. Not many people were out yet, just a few other walkers and an occasional jogger passing by.

The beaches were empty now, although later, they'd be filled with families enjoying their day.

This morning, I was walking towards the coast that is lined with homes on top of the bluff. There was a new home under construction in front of me and I tilted my head up to look at it.

It was at that moment that I sensed a bullet hit me on my lower forehead between my eyes and I knew it blew a large chunk out of the back of my head as it exited. I knew instantly what had happened and where it had happened. I had just had a spontaneous past life memory of my death on the beach of Normandy, France at H-Hour on D-Day, June 6, 1944!

This wasn't just my imagination creating something. It felt as valid as reality. My visceral reaction to this experience, deep within my body, proved to me it was real. My subconscious was releasing the painful energy stored in every cell. I began to cry. Not just watery eyes, I cried like never before and I couldn't stop. It got to the point that I was worried someone I knew would see me. When I finally regained control of myself, I wiped away the tears with my shirt.

I was confused about what had just happened. It wasn't until later that I heard the term "spontaneous past life memory."

I had to share this with someone, but I wasn't sure with whom. Most people I knew would think I was crazy. Heck, *I* thought I was crazy. But I remembered a conversation from more than a year earlier about past lives and my experience in this lifetime at Normandy.

I had been working with a woman who was helping me remove subconscious blocks. During one of our last sessions, the topic of past lives came up. I told her I had read that if someone had an interest in certain historical eras, cultures, or fashion they may have had a past life during that timeline. She agreed and asked me about my interest in history. We discussed historical eras including Ancient Egypt, the American Civil War, and World War II.

I told her about my vacation to France years prior. My wife at the time knew I wanted to see the landing beaches at Normandy, which coincided with her interest in a visit to nearby Mont St Michel. During that trip we stayed in the village of Bayeux, which was central to these sites. The morning of our visit, we piled into the rental car and drove to the Normandy American Cemetery at Coleville-sur-Mer.

There were placards to read explaining the landings and I was sharing my knowledge with the family. We walked past many of the thousands of graves and read the names, ranks, and home states as well as the dates of death on the crosses and Stars of David.

One of my children asked if we could go down to the beach. We headed to the edge of the cemetery, which is lined with trees and a path, and found a wooden staircase that led down the bluff to the beach.

I suddenly stopped about halfway down the stairs, turned to my ex, and said, "I'm going to stay here."

She looked at me a bit sideways. "You're going to stay here?"

"Yes, I'm just going to watch you from here."

My ex shrugged and they continued to the beach. The rest of my family walked and laughed. I saw them stick their toes in the freezing cold Channel waters. I watched.

I concluded my story to Bev by saying, "I love the beach. This wasn't normal behavior for me. I grew up on the beach in Southern California."

Bev told me that I had been there and that I had witnessed so much carnage, destruction, and death that I didn't want to experience it again. At the time, this made sense to me. I left it alone and we moved on to other historical interests.

After having my spontaneous past life memory, I realized that Bev was the one to talk to about it. I called her the next day and recounted the experience. There was silence at her end of the line. She said that she remembered having discussed my vacation to France and she simply said, "Mark, I didn't mean to lie to you, but I didn't think you needed to know that you had died on that beach."

She said it in a very heartfelt genuine way, and I believed her.

I was so grateful that I hadn't gone down to the beach that day with my family. I can't imagine the feelings of fear and confusion that they might have experienced had they witnessed my spontaneous past life memory and my reaction there.

Since that day, I have learned more about that lifetime via past life regressions and psychic readings. I have seen more details of that infamous day. Scenes of climbing down the sides of grey metal ships on makeshift ladders made of cargo nets and jumping into the landing crafts. The LCs circling in rough seas until they were all loaded, and the formation was ready to head to the beach. The coxswains were confused and lost, but they did their best to get us to our intended landing points.

I saw myself leading my platoon onto the beach until I was hit. I heard the noises of battle: screams, shouts, and explosions peppered by that unique sound of the German machine guns firing short, fast bursts.

I remembered falling backwards from the momentum of the German MG-41 bullet that hit me, then rising out of my body and watching the scene from above, noticing that there were other souls watching from above as well. I was still giving out orders and encouragement until I realized that they weren't being heard, and I had to move onwards.

Soul awakenings can happen in different ways. This event was my awakening. It was the beginning of my following a road less traveled and the past lives that I've discovered weave a web that is the story of my soul.

Someday, I plan to go back to Normandy to finish that walk down the beach to the waterline. I'll wade out a distance and then turn around and face the bluff.

Mark McAdams

ADVENTURES IN INFINITY

"I am a failure." I repeated the discouraging phrase aloud in a soft voice.

My practitioner, using all her skills in applied kinesiology, pressed down on my arm, to check my mind-body resonance with that statement. She had unearthed an old belief that was stuck somewhere in the craw of my unconscious mind.

My arm stayed strong, firm as a rock. An unknown part of my body-mind system was holding onto this ancient belief, like a retriever dog with its bone, unwilling to give it up.

I was shocked. *When did this happen?* I wondered.

My practitioner, Hilda, muscle-checked. Present life? No. Past life? Yes. How many years ago? She counted back, muscle-checking the centuries.

"Ahh, in the 9th century. Let's see. Your caste? Hmmm. Warrior/Priest," she affirmed, muscle-checking throughout, "and you were male in that lifetime." She looked directly at me, asking casually, "Now, where would that have been?"

As if a banner were floating through my mind, letters appeared, one at time, slowly spelling out a word: I C E L A N D...

"Iceland?" I responded, incredulously.

She affirmed that it was so. Using her expertise in vibrational modalities, we shifted my resonance with the statement and cleared that belief at the level of awareness available to us at that time. As the session ended, I was relieved that I no longer resonated with that subconscious thought-form. And then I didn't really think about it much more. Until…

About six months later, I was driving to Phoenix, Arizona from Santa Fe, New Mexico, for the annual conference of the healing art that Hilda and I both practiced. Heading down Interstate I-40, in the middle of the desert somewhere between Gallup and Holbrook, I began to experience bizarre, excruciating stomach pains. My guts felt like they were twisting and spasming in a way I'd never felt before.

Outside my car, the muted pink, orange, and purple-colored formations of the Painted Desert gleamed in the hot midday sun. There was no rest area or gas station available for miles. The only thing to do, I decided, was to keep driving and to breathe into the pain and try to feel what was causing it.

I began breathing deeply, focusing on the uncomfortable sensations. As if I were experiencing retrograde amnesia, I began seeing flashes of images in bright, internal colors. Golden green hills, somewhere far away. . . a male warrior, marching, leading a small group of men into battle. That was me!

I'd been confident that we would easily win, but instead, our troop was ambushed. My past life self was dragged off to the enemy camp, where in vivid detail, I could see myself being tortured to death.

My bilocated consciousness saw that on one hand, I was driving seventy-five miles an hour through the Painted Desert, but on the other hand, in my inner vision, I saw how I, in that past life, had been disemboweled and my guts wrapped around a tree. This technique was a typical Viking way of torturing people to death. Worse than the pain and the shame was the fact that I could sense, with my inner eye, that all my men had been captured or killed.

As the vision slowly disappeared, so did the stomachache. It was completely gone. I felt fine, just shaken up.

No wonder my ancient memories held the belief that "I was a failure." I had gotten all my men killed in battle.

Over time, the memory slowly faded away, as new, exciting experiences filled my life. One of those events was a chance to spend winters on a friend's farm in Hawaii. Living near the beach and creating a verdant oasis of kukui nut trees, coconut palms, and dragon fruit was a great antidote to enduring the winters in the cold, parched high desert where I lived.

Eleven years later, on the island of Kauai, I met my life partner, Gregory. We were working together to help build a permaculture garden there on my friend's farm. As the exciting passion of new love filled my soul, I was thrilled. I had been waiting to meet "the one," and here he was.

One sultry, tropical afternoon, listening to the sounds of the banana leaves rustling in the breeze, Greg and I started snuggling in my tent. We finally began what I had been yearning for: exploring one another's bodies. Warm, passionate kisses, flesh on flesh, the soft glow of sweat melting our bodies together…

But suddenly, I burst into loud sobs, my tears erupting out of nowhere.

"What's happening?" Greg asked, considerably concerned and mystified at what was derailing our intimate tryst. "What's the matter? What's wrong, Marya?"

"I'm having a flashback, Greg! I think got you killed!" I started wailing.

While my body was in the tent with Greg, my mind was experiencing the vivid memory of Greg and me when we were in different bodies, both male. I was the captain of that small warrior band, back in that lifetime in Iceland in the 9th century. I clearly "saw" in my vision that Greg had been my right-hand man, my captain-at-arms, and my best buddy.

I was thrown into that same, dreadful "instant replay" of the event that had surfaced during the excruciating stomachache on Interstate 40, eleven years earlier. I watched the vision unfold in blood-curdling detail once more: We were boldly marching off to attack and obliterate our rival gang, but in a mismatched skirmish, they ambushed us from behind a low ring of hills, in a pea-soup fog. They killed all my men, captured me, dragged me to the enemy camp, and tortured me to death.

But what had happened to Greg in that life? I couldn't quite make it out, but I knew it wasn't good. I was hoping he hadn't been killed outright, garroted by the enemy band during the ambush. Perhaps he had been captured, too? Oh, but that would be worse. I couldn't discover what happened. The vision fizzled out right at that point. And that's when I started crying.

Greg responded to my flashback very well. Stroking my back and holding me tightly, he reassured me he was here. He had come back again, and we had another chance. Eventually I could take a deep breath once more and my confused sobbing ceased. I came back to the present time, grateful that he was back in my life once more and we were together again.

Gregory and I were able to spend nine amazing years together and experience other mystical events. We survived the entire gamut of trials and tribulations of daily life in the third dimension, in a relationship on the cusp of the new millennium. Love, fights, despair, adventures, international travel, transcendent moments—we had it all. We experienced much, and we learned how to forgive one another and ourselves. He was my best buddy once more.

In September 2016, I was broken apart when Greg disappeared and died in a mysterious accident. Once again, as in that past life, I did not get to say goodbye to him. But two months after his death, as I attended a healing meditation, his radiant soul came floating in from the beyond on a shaft of golden light. He connected to my soul through a beam of pure love rising powerfully from my heart chakra. We were able to share a healing embrace and express our unconditional love, one more time.

His death, though tragic, was not the end of his essence. And it was not the end of our relationship and connectedness through space and time.

I know in my heart of hearts, my soul of souls, that we will have another rendezvous and more adventures somewhere down the amazing avenues of space and time.

The wisdom of Source had woven our life paths to connect again, an irrevocable tapestry of love, destiny, free will, and forgiveness. And thanks to that Great Mystery, I know that I am not a failure.

Marya Corneli

THE MYSTICAL HEATH

Standing on a deep sandy path in Northern Germany's famous Lueneburg Heath Nature Park, I felt an indescribable connection to the local landscape, which seemed a wonder to me as an exchange student from America. Rolling, sandy hills were interspersed with clumps of tall green grasses and plentiful heather plants, their deep purple stems cloaking the hills in vibrant color.

The heather blossom's intoxicating sweet scent hung in the air. The stunning views were interrupted only by an errant pine or silvery birch tree, with a strip of deep green brush and trees on the far horizon. Suddenly, I became rooted to the heathland as a pulsing energy began to be emitted from the sandy path. The sensation reached up through my feet, into my legs, torso, and heart. I stood there as if alone, the fellow hikers in this vast area fading from awareness while I connected deeply to the land, and its timeless whispers.

The lure of Germany first captured me as an 11-year-old who found the language easy to learn. Fascinated with German culture, heritage, and history, I was fortunate to spend a high school summer in Northern Germany as an American Field Service exchange student, where I soon felt like I was home.

Up until the nature park visit, life on a small dairy farm had seemed simple, yet fulfilling. I enjoyed helping my host family make daily excursions to milk their small herd of white and black Holstein cows by hand as they grazed in nearby pastures. I appreciated the century-old farm with its combination house and barn under one enormous, straw-thatched roof. And the land that was so flat that one could see to the horizon over the small, lush pastures of nearby families, see to where the deep green grass met the clear, robin-egg blue sky.

My host sister and instant good friend was just a year older than I on this warm August day. The wide tires of our heavy, old bicycles hummed with purpose as early in the morning we peddled down narrow country roads that carried few automobiles, cherishing our freedom from farm work and adult supervision. We sped to catch a train from the nearby village, sneezing and laughing while inhaling the fragrance of freshly cut hay and shouting "Moo!" at grazing cows in lush, green pastures. It was exciting to venture to Lueneburg Heath, the largest of its kind in Central Europe, stretching from Oldenburg to Bremen to Hannover.

Once aboard a train to a neighboring town near the famed Heath, we settled into its gentle swaying rhythm as we spied cotton-ball clouds out the windows that drifted slowly above us in a bright blue sky, their shapes slowly casting playful shadows upon everything below.

Because no cars were allowed in the heathland area, we linked arms upon arrival and strode off, our feet sinking into the warming sands of the path leading to the amethyst-bejeweled hills ahead. A pair of stocky ponies whose coats matched the path color surprised us with their camouflage as they crested the first hill we reached. Their broad heads hung low, eyes hidden by their long forelocks that floated up and down with each step. Attached to the ponies was a small wooden wagon bearing tourists, and we stepped aside to let the ponies with their gentle four-beat cadence and wobbly wagon load pass by.

The intense August sun bore down on us for the first hours of walking into the beauty of the rolling, tufted, blooming landscape. Small herds of shaggy Heidschnucke sheep appeared around a bend, roaming at will across the heathland while grazing upon wayward weeds and tree shoots. The sheep barely raised their heads as we strode by, our shoes coated with glittering golden sand like pixie dust.

One could feel Mother Nature's presence here, singing to her fields of heather and laughing at the shaggy sheep munching the day away. The mystery, the life power of the Heath, caused me to suddenly stop as I felt a shift, a type of mental swoon. The pulsing energy from the path rose in my body as the people on neighboring paths disappeared from my vision. The Heath itself shape-shifted, transporting me to another time.

I was on these same hills, but without the walking paths. Larger birch and pine trees had sprung up before me, clustered haphazardly around the borders of the heath fields and within them. I looked down, bewildered that my feet now sported coarsely carved wooden clogs with blunt tips that peeked out from underneath a long, dark, plain skirt.

My dazed mind picked up a lovely, soft whisper of *Remember!*

Remember what? I silently replied. But to whom?

Remember! The whisper commanded me. *Remember!*

Visions swept over me, as I stood still, trembling. I had walked this heath many times before in various lifetimes. I was the young peasant girl in a dark skirt and wooden shoes, gathering firewood and picking sprigs of heather to sell at a market to help feed my family. I saw myself searching among the trees for small fallen branches, which snapped loudly as I broke them for bundling to carry home. My hands were dirty and calloused, and my nails were torn in jagged edges. The bundle of sticks weighed upon my shoulders and back, and broken branch tips dug into my skin through the loose blouse. The fragrance of the pines and heather blossoms filled my nostrils.

Then the Heath appeared to rise in a waving roll, changing the landscape and showing a vision of myself as a teenage boy in tattered pants that reached only to my calves. Looking down as the boy, I saw wrinkled, old hand-me-down leather boots that were much too large for me. The cold iron of a long gun was in my arms, with my grip tight on the wooden stock as I tripped over the primitive trails from the oversized boots making it slow going. From hunger in my belly, I knew that I was hunting for rabbits on the rolling hills.

The Heath shifted yet again, and the air moved around me. Gazing about, I made out the shapes of uniformed German soldiers brushing past me into the deepening twilight as they crushed the fragile landscape, marching onward to another conflict. One soldier stopped right before me, his back to me. His long, woolen coat of gray was draped over the grasses and heather. He turned and his gaze startled me, seeming to look right at or through me. Suddenly, I felt myself moving forward with him as he turned and marched to catch up with the others. I was now a soldier in this patrol, full of fear, hunger, thirst, and exhaustion as my booted feet bore me forward. The only sounds came from the grasses being flattened by our boots, and an occasional clink of a metal canteen hitting against belts and guns.

Remember! the whispering voice insisted.

"Cheri?" I heard my name being spoken louder, and close to my ears.

The sound brought me back from my sleep-like journey to a foggy awareness of my own body, and of a woman talking to me. I turned to my host sister. Apparently, she had asked a question that I missed.

"Ja?" I finally croaked, still wanting to keep the mystical feelings and visions with me.

Yet I had been pulled out of the Heath's embrace. The Heath had let me go after fulfilling her goal to help me remember.

Once again, I noticed older women in sturdy skirts with walking staffs on the nearby paths as my vision refocused on my 16-year-old self's surroundings. I was back in virtually the same place and time based on their positions on the path. What had seemed like an hour of visions to me must have lasted just a few seconds.

Despite being dazed, I managed to return more fully to the present time as we retraced a pathway back to our starting point and I began processing my visit to the mystical Heath. I spoke nothing of my experience to my host sister, deciding to keep this special memory private. It was a gift to me from the Heath, and I cherished it.

The Heath had reminded me of previous lives and, to return that honor, I struck upon the perfect idea before drifting off to sleep that night. In repayment to the Heath for opening my eyes to mysticism, I promised that, if I ever had a daughter, her name would be Heather. And so, I now have a living memorial to the Heath, as well as everlasting gratitude for the landscape that helped me remember my eternal self.

Cheri Evjen

CRYSTALLINE TEMPLE IN ATLANTIS

As we embarked on a whale watching excursion on a bay on the Sea of Cortez in Baja California, Mexico, the morning greeted us with flawless blue skies, filling our group with anticipation. The ocean stretched before us in serene tranquility, its gentle blue surface inviting us to venture forth on our adventure.

Upon reaching a particular area of the breathtaking bay, my inner vision revealed an extraordinary sight: a colossal crystalline pyramid standing gracefully on the ocean's surface. Its transparent structure refracted light into delicate pastel hues—soft pink, gold, turquoise, and white—that danced across its surface. I sensed its vibrations extending throughout the entire bay, reaching the nearby mountains. An unmistakable call to stillness washed over me, drawing me inward as I recognized an ancient, profound connection to this ethereal structure—a bond that seemed to transcend time itself.

Ancient knowledge stirred within. I started remembering.

Standing atop a precipitous cliff, I gazed out over a small horseshoe-shaped bay where tranquil ocean waters met the shore. Narrow stone stairways zigzagged down the cliff's steep face toward the slender strip of beach below. As my eyes traced the shoreline where sand met sea, an extraordinary vision unfolded—a massive crystalline pyramid materializing above the water's surface.

The magnificent structure towered high, surpassing even the cliff's formidable height. Its translucent faces caught the light, and I felt so much joy and wonder.

I descended rapidly yet deliberately down the narrow stairway toward the numerous caverns embedded within the cliff face. After a brief journey, I arrived at a particular grotto that resonated with deep familiarity—my personal sanctuary. Though modest in size, resembling more a comfortable chamber than an expansive cave, it enveloped me in its distinctive atmosphere. The palpable dampness mingled with the fragrant essences of aromatic oils and fresh blossoms that I had carefully placed throughout.

Crystalline formations and various stones adorned every surface. Nestled in one corner stood my crystal altar, adorned with a collection of meaningful treasures: vibrant flowers, delicate seashells, a carved whale figurine, a wooden ankh symbol, assorted small keepsakes, and a single candle.

I settled into a small, cushioned ottoman chair, its fabric worn smooth from years of use. Without hesitation, I removed my simple cotton blouse and reached for a ceremonial gown. The fabric felt cool against my skin as I draped it over my frock, its considerable weight both comforting and familiar. Intricate patterns of tiny gemstones adorned the edges and swirled across the material in mesmerizing designs.

I exchanged my footwear for worn golden sandals and carefully positioned a delicate headdress of shells and crystals upon my long, auburn locks. As I arranged my wavy tresses, I noticed strands of silver threading through the dark copper curls.

With a sense of urgency, I hastened along the path toward the beach, making my way to the pyramid. After reaching the shoreline, I discovered a gathering of women already assembled, each adorned in light blue ceremonial robes resembling my own, though less elaborately embellished.

They welcomed me with joyful, yet earnest greetings, and then promptly formed a line facing the crystalline pyramid rising from the water. They had saved a space for me precisely at the center of their formation. The gentle ocean waves lapped at our feet, sending cool ripples of seawater across our skin.

In that moment, recognition dawned, I was the High Priestess of this ethereal, multi-dimensional structure in ancient Atlantis. These women were my fellow priestesses, thirteen of us in total. I could feel our collective energy aligning, our presence activating a powerful resonance that harmonized with the temple pyramid's elevated frequencies.

With gentle harmony, our voices rose in unified tones. I initiated a sacred melody, my hands flowing through precise ritual gestures resembling ancient mudras. Our bodies began to sway rhythmically with our chanting, each of us immersed in the profound sanctity of the moment.

I realized the pyramid temple stood farther from shore than it had appeared from the clifftop perspective. After a period of ceremonial preparation, I began the approach, stepping deliberately into the waters. As I waded deeper, the remarkable occurred—with each step, the water beneath my feet subtly solidified, creating an unseen pathway that lovingly supported my journey toward the temple.

Upon reaching the magnificent structure, I entered reverently through an opening in one of its crystalline faces, feeling an immediate sense of belonging. Gazing upward into the temple's soaring interior, I offered a gesture of deep veneration to the conscious essence of the pyramid, my heart overflowing with gratitude for the privilege of once again entering this sacred space to serve alongside and in partnership with the living crystalline sanctuary.

This structure's visible portion formed a four-sided pyramid above the water's surface. Yet my inner vision revealed its complete geometry: an octahedral formation with a second, inverted pyramid extending beneath the water's surface, joining at their square bases. Being etheric in nature, this temple transcended material constraints, emanating subtle, pulsating energy waves from its core that radiated outward in all directions.

I understood instinctively that this sacred structure possessed remarkable qualities of adaptation—able to shift its position within the bay and transform its dimensions according to energetic requirements and cosmic alignments.

Once all the priestesses had entered, we assembled in a circle at the precise center of the crystalline temple's energetic vortex. From the oceanic depths came the distinctive whistles and clicks of approaching dolphins. The pod surrounded us joyfully, creating a second, dynamic circle as they swam continuously around our formation. We exchanged silent greetings of pure heart-connection with these magnificent beings.

From beneath the water's surface at the center of our circle, a radiant golden-white light began to form. It grew steadily in brightness and dimension until a massive transparent crystal—faceted and semi-rounded like quartz—emerged mysteriously from the water. The luminous formation hovered weightlessly above the surface, suspended over the ocean.

At once, the priestesses and I began intoning a new melodic sequence. Our voices harmonized, creating vibrations that resonated with the crystalline structure, initiating a two-way quantum communication. I felt profound connections forming—to the geometric temple, to the heart of the hovering crystal with its exquisite radiance, to the water, and to all elemental forces. Simultaneously, I sensed my own internal octahedral energy field activating, my crystalline heart center beginning to vibrate in resonance.

Together, we linked our higher heart energies to one another and to the central crystal. Our awareness expanded both upward and downward through our energetic bodies, aligning perfectly with the apex and nadir points of the pyramid. Complete synchronicity enveloped us.

As our chanting continued, I observed the interior walls of the pyramid with heightened perception. The structure was visibly pulsating with subtle rhythmic movements. Various shimmering lights began manifesting—delicate pastel hues resembling a soft rainbow spectrum with opalescent qualities. Golden symbols resembling ancient scrolls materialized along specific locations on the walls, accompanied by intricate patterns that appeared to be a form of light language.

A whale's song resonated through the water as a majestic mother whale approached, joining our sacred gathering. She entered our circle, gliding with deliberate grace around the suspended, golden-white crystal. Drawn by our energetic call, other beings arrived to lend their support—mer-people, star families, inhabitants from inner earth, sea turtles, and various other beings.

For what purpose were we summoning such diverse cosmic assistance?

A sudden shock jolted me as my 21st century self, experienced a profound revelation. In that moment, I understood the purpose behind our gathering, the reason for this unified call across dimensions and species. The urgency of the hour and the knowingness of that timeline took hold of me. I felt profound sorrow. The collapse of Atlantis was imminent.

United in purpose, we reached out with the purest intentions of our hearts, beseeching Spirit for intervention—desperately seeking to alter the catastrophic path that lay before our civilization. I sensed the profound grief permeating all realms of existence, including our own spirits. A desperate question was present: Could we somehow prevent the suffering about to befall countless living beings? Was there still time to right the course of our shared destiny?

A growing assembly outside the crystalline temple was gathering—marine creatures of all varieties and birds of countless species coming together near the structure. They responded to both the mournful invocation and the profound beauty of our unified presence across dimensional boundaries. Our collective energy formed a powerful plea for Divine intervention.

Despite the weight of emotion, I maintained my composure, recognizing the critical importance of remaining centered and focused to sustain the energetic process we had initiated. The pyramid temple resonated in perfect symbiosis with our presence; its consciousness aligned with our sacred purpose.

A brilliant ray of golden-white light burst from the central crystal, extending vertically in both directions to connect with the apex and nadir of the pyramid structure. This luminous beam stretched skyward toward the heavens and simultaneously downward into the heart of Gaia herself.

We fell into deep silence, reflecting reverence and prayer, our hearts clinging to fragile hope. Yet deep within my being, I recognized the inevitable truth—the final hour had arrived, and the cosmic decision had already been made. Whether our efforts came too late or this outcome served some greater purpose beyond our understanding, I could not say. The grief was so overwhelming, so hollow, so absolute that it seemed to transcend time itself.

Even now, as I revisit that moment and what followed, the raw emotion remains—the anguish as vivid within me today as it was in that ancient time.

I have now reconciled with this profound trauma. I have released the deep sorrow and heartbreak and the grief for all that was lost: my beloved ones, the land, and every living being of Atlantis. I have finally let go of the burden of guilt and shame that weighed on me for not accomplishing more.

With greater wisdom now, I have embraced this chapter as an integral part of my soul's journey. The key is compassionate and loving acceptance.

Monica Alonso

A FARMER IN 1800s EUROPE

*I*n 2014, my father, Ivan, was in his ninth year of care in a psychiatric geriatric facility for people with advanced dementia. My sister Sonia and I would visit every weekend to feed him lunch. Visits usually included an array of emotions ranging from tears of anguish to the thrill of laughter.

As Ivan's cognitive decline deepened, we would often reminisce, repeating stories of our childhood, those narratives that thread the juxtaposition of both harmony and complications familiar to many families.

Verbal sparring had been a popular pastime for Ivan. Growing up, our mother wryly called our family evening gathering at the meal table "happy hour." Yet despite the cognitive degeneration of his brain, Ivan's eyes reflected in fleeting moments what we considered understanding. We believed his soul was a constant and present observer of his human experience—as with all of us.

That year, I decided to see Glenda, a qualified practitioner, for a past life reading. I went into the experience with excited anticipation, as I was not too sure of what to expect. A previous reading with an evidential medium had inspired me. That medium had noted that my maternal grandmother, Betty

Rita, had been my mother in a previous life and that my current mother and I had been sisters in that life.

The reading opened with Glenda talking me into a relaxed state, asking me to recall a happy early childhood memory. From an observational viewpoint, I watched five-year-old Sonia chasing my toddler self in the shallows of Melbourne's bayside, St. Kilda beach. Our mother stood ankle-deep in the water watching us. She wore a checked bikini and was sporting a teased, bee-hive hairstyle. Our father was inattentive, sitting in a deck chair, reading a newspaper.

Glenda then took me to the time while I was still in utero. I expressed feeling content in the nurturing warmth of the womb. I knew I was wanted. However, I could feel my mother's anxiety and the bereft emptiness of mourning. Her mother, Betty Rita, had died unexpectedly a week before I was born.

Hopping onto a cushioning and comforting cloud to travel further back, Glenda proposed that I next enter a past life of my soul's choosing, one with relevance to my current life.

A visual promptly appeared of me standing in what I described as a large field of tiny, sprouting green shoots. I was in my fifties. Experiencing the scene rather than observing, I felt immense pride in this lone accomplishment.

Glenda then directed my attention to notice what I was wearing. Looking down at my feet, I had leather slip-on shoes. I wore a heavily pleated, full-length skirt with a three-quarter apron wrapped around my stout and ample waist. I had short, silvery-blond, graying hair.

Across the field stood a solidly built, white-washed brick or stone house with a tiled terra cotta roof. Behind the house stood a thick patch of deep green forest. I sensed it was somewhere in the early 1800s in Eastern Europe. Poland came to mind.

I felt uneasy. The house should have had people in it, but it was empty. I preferred to be outside in the field rather than in the house, feeling a strong connection to the land and place. I sensed I was part of a small, rural village community. Despite my achievement, I felt a pervasive sense of loneliness. The house was cold, dark, and empty.

The regressionist asked me to go back to an earlier moment in this life.

I was transported to a kitchen scene, perhaps ten years earlier. It was evening and the warm amber glow from an open fireplace lit the kitchen. The peripheral parts of the room were dim.

It was a double-story house with a ceiling quite low by modern standards. Heavy wooden beams added to the enclosed feeling, though the hues offered a comfortable intimacy. I was dressed as I had been in the field and was lifting a roasted bird from the oven. I rested it on an oval platter adorned with vegetables creating an enticing centerpiece on the long, narrow wooden table. I declared it a time of abundance, a festive celebration.

Standing around were perhaps a dozen people I identified as members of the community. They were all adults, and the atmosphere was of ample merriment. This sizeable room was flowing with conversation as people drank wine from caramel-colored, ceramic goblets.

Seated around the table were members of my family, including two adolescents, my son and daughter—and my husband. Strangely, I could not see him. He was a simple gray silhouette, like a cardboard cut-out. I did note that my attention was drawn more to the community members than to my family. It was a happy time, I concluded.

With nothing else to report, Glenda prompted me to go back to a still earlier time in this life, and my wedding day presented. I looked about twenty-three years old, and I was sitting on a bench next to my husband. We leaned against a dull, dusky pink wall.

Observing myself from approximately three feet away, I could see I wore a simple, summery white dress. My long, auburn hair was loose. I saw my face in profile as I was facing my husband, except he was a silhouette—just a shadow sitting next to me.

A strong emotion emerged as I announced, "I have no emotional connection to my husband … we are from the same village … there was no coercion to marry him … I feel absolutely nothing for him … I got married because it was just something that we did."

And with that, it dawned on me that my husband in that life—is my father in this life.

When I had no further details to offer about the wedding day, Glenda asked me to go to the day of my death. My soul transported me back to the opening scene. As the specifics of my death were not revealed, Glenda asked me to identify who met me when I died. My maternal grandmother of this life, Betty Rita, appeared. I asked her where Mum was—my mother in this life—and a fifteen-year-old version of Mum appeared. In that moment, both women enveloped me in total acceptance and love. I felt absolutely fine about leaving my body. I probably dropped dead in that field. I don't sense I lived to an old age. I laughed.

And herein lies the confirmation of soul groups incarnating across multiple lives, which weave across decades of synchronicities to meet again in this one human lifetime of experience—this contribution to my soul's expansion.

And of my father Ivan?

It occurred to me that I had driven my husband away. I suppose it was because I did not give him the love that he needed. I understood now that this resulted in an estrangement with my adult children in that life. I had lost connection with my family. While I was proud of my independence, surviving as a single woman with a successful crop sprouting, the loneliness required unexpected emotional endurance. The house was now empty and cold because it was devoid of people.

I identified empathy as a key lesson of that life.

This past life reveal spoke to me about emotional complications Ivan and I carried through to this incarnation. I continue to collaborate with my ancestral team and guides to energetically heal those wounds, across all our lives, in all timelines.

And so it is.

Simone Senisin

THE EGYPTIAN CONNECTION

I n 2010, I attended a music program at a Unity Church in Novato, California. One of the presenting musicians shared that she was planning to be in Egypt for 11-11-11 (November 11, 2011). A native Egyptian archeologist would also be one of the tour leaders.

I have always loved music, and having a sound healer on the trip made my heart sing! I've long been interested in sacred sites, and being in a group led by an Egyptian archeologist would offer insight and perspective on the different locations. I was thrilled to sign up for this trip!

As I prepared for the trip and big adventure, everything seemed effortless. However, the Egyptian political unrest that unfolded in February 2011 cast a shadow on our plans. Many tour groups canceled their planned trips.

Our tour group proceeded with the travel plans, reassured that the trip would be canceled if it was not safe to proceed. This unique situation had an unexpected benefit for our group to visit places without the usual large crowds of people. We were also able to go to places that many visitors seldom see.

In early November of 2011, I boarded a flight from New York City to Cairo. The first few days we explored Cairo, the pyramids of Giza, and the

Sphinx. We rode camels and saw the treasures within the city's Egyptian Museum. We continued to explore major historical sites traveling by bus, jeep, plane, and boats.

On 11-11-11, our Nile River cruise ship was docked in Aswan. In the morning, we took a small, traditional felucca wooden boat to the west side of the Nile and explored an ancient site. While we gathered under a thatched roof cover to take a break, I felt immersed in the history of the setting and heard the calls for prayer from the tall surrounding Mosque towers.

As I sat there, my body started to circle. I began to speak, and a deeper, wiser, and more intentional voice emerged from my mouth. My body was running a different and higher energy current, and I felt that I had once been part of this land.

We once again rode the felucca boat across the Nile River to have lunch at the historic Old Cataract Aswan Hotel. I let my Egyptian ankh cross skim the waters of the Nile, as if to infuse the pendant with droplets of Egyptian history.

Following our lovely lunch on this memorable day, we embarked on another felucca boat ride. Egyptian musicians played their instruments as we sailed to the small island of Philae to explore the revered Temple of Isis.

The guards proceeded to lead us to a special site beyond the public areas. From that site, we were able to have our ceremony with the reassurance to the guards that our intention was to celebrate and honor the people and land of Egypt. We took turns as individuals going around our group circle sharing blessings.

When it was my turn, I started crying tears of joy. I was in an ecstatic state. I stopped in front of a woman, making motions with my hands and then gently patting her feet, as if to ground her into the experience.

Later, this woman told me that when I had stopped in front of her, she'd had a vision of me being a high priestess and healer in an ancient Egyptian era. The experience was both magical and mystical. It was validating that my soul had called me to return to this sacred place and remember a part of my pedigree as both a healer and seer between two worlds.

Following our ceremony within the grounds of the Temple of Isis, the guards became our guides as they personally led us through the ancient structures. The brilliant yellow and orange sunset made the setting memorable, and we knew the night before us would be lit by a full moon shining its light upon the Nile.

We each returned home from this adventure filled with introspection about all we had experienced. It had been more meaningful than we could ever have imagined before the trip.

In this lifetime, I worked as a nurse for forty-three years, incorporating both traditional and non-traditional interventions with my patients. In my later work years, one of my passions was being involved with palliative care. I helped facilitate bereavement weekends and programs for the families I worked with. Like the ancient Egyptians, I became very interested in the afterlife.

I am now shifting to more spiritual healing as I study spiritual mediumship and become a voice between the two worlds. The Egyptian connection helped reinforce and validate how my soul has chosen to share its soul gifts in both past and present lifetimes with healing and coming full circle to surrender to awe, mystery, and love.

Leslie Griffith

UNLUCKY IN LOVE

S hortly after completing college, I moved from Washington State to sunny California. Interactions with new friends led to fun-filled beach days, enjoyable restaurant dining, and nights out at nightclubs.

During one of those hot summers, my friends and I became fans of a favorite band, and after flirting a bit, I began dating the drummer. David was charming, fun, extremely talented, and a very handsome Lothario.

Soon, we began living together. I was a young, naive gal, and David was eight years older, occupying his time with ladies, drugs, and rock and roll. As our lives became increasingly entangled, the relationship began to become more dysfunctional. I moved out several times, but there was always a gravitational force that pulled me back, feeling like he needed me, and I needed him.

I bought him a car, cut his hair, and even helped him find a day job. Two steps forward, thirty steps backward and we repeatedly did the "I'm leaving... I will never do it again... let's make it work" cha-cha.

I was confused and depressed. I desperately needed a life change. Over time, I'd been growing up and getting wiser, but he hadn't.

One day, while running errands, I stumbled upon a metaphysical bookstore, which piqued my interest. After perusing the aisles, I found myself in the back of the store looking at a bulletin board where pieces of paper and business cards had been randomly tacked up, soliciting all types of business opportunities. One card in particular caught my attention. It belonged to a psychotherapist card and read, "Challenge unhealthy patterns of thinking and behavior through past life regression."

The idea of a past life regression was intriguing, and I was so desperate that I would have tried anything to change my life. I took that card and, without any further hesitation, made the call.

To this day, I still remember seeing Dr. Tan's gentle face as he opened the door to his office. He was a small-framed, gray-haired man with a quiet demeanor and extremely kind blue eyes.

At first, we discussed my relationship concerns. He sympathized with the "life pothole" I had managed to get myself into. This man was so kind and loving that I intuitively trusted him. He asked me to lie on a comfortable couch covered by wonderfully warm blankets.

Dr. Tan began coaching me into a quiet and relaxing state. I could feel my body sinking deeper into an abyss of peace and tranquility. I could hear Dr. Tan's faint voice in my ear: "Go back to the lifetime that has had the most significant impact on today's circumstances."

With my eyes closed and my mind's eye wide open, I instantly felt the sun's warm rays fall upon my cheeks as I gazed up at a beautiful blue sky dotted with white fluffy clouds. I stood in the middle of an expansive green field where the warm, wet grass tickled my bare feet. At the edge of this magical expanse was a drastic drop-off into the ocean, as if God had used a blade and abruptly sliced away the land.

I was a little girl, probably about five years old, wearing a plain, worn-out muslin dress. I looked down at my little body, familiarizing myself with the tiny, frail frame. I enjoyed running and frolicking in this field, knowing this was my home, my land. I lived right at the edge of nowhere.

I could hear Dr. Tan's voice encouraging me to move forward in time. Instantly, I was looking at a much older version of myself, roughly thirteen or fourteen years of age. I was on the same plot of land, but not alone this time. A strange man approached me. He seemed very nice, cooing his way into my trusting heart. Suddenly, my clothes were being ripped off and I was thrown to the ground. I remembered the feeling of being helplessly confused and begging him to stop.

Realizing my agitation, Dr. Tan quickly moved me forward in time. He would periodically remind me that I was safe and only an observer, which was an instant, healing balm.

Once again, I moved into the future of that same past life. Immediately, I saw myself cowering in the corner of a tiny, rustic cabin. Feelings of extreme sadness and fear wafted over me. I watched my past life self as I sobbed uncontrollably, shielding my face with my scrawny arms while watching my father in a rage. He turned over an old, worn-out table, catapulting hand carved wooden bowls through the air. I realized that, after the altercation with the stranger, I had come home beaten and bruised. My father was beside himself feeling angry, helpless, and out of control.

Dr. Tan's soothing voice moved me into the future again. I now stood at a crude-looking window inside the same small, dreary cabin. I drew the curtains back and tried to wave as I sadly smiled at a boy about four or five years of age. With his jet-black hair under a wide-brimmed, black hat, he wildly and joyfully waved back as he sat on the back of an old wooden cart, his frail legs dangling off the edge. A man sat in the front of the cart, slapping an old horse with reins, encouraging it to move forward.

Intuitively, I knew his boy was my son. I had given birth, which was the consequence of my rape. With great despair, I knew if my son were to stay on the farm, we could not afford to care for him—we have no means, money, or future. With a hollowness in my heart, I knew I would never see him again.

"Heather, do you recognize anyone in your past life that might be in this current life?" Dr. Tan prompted.

I immediately knew that the beautiful baby boy was my current boyfriend, David. In that lifetime, I had been consumed with guilt and regret for sending him away.

As I emerged from the regression, I felt complete peace and a newfound confidence in making a life change. What an excellent way to gain such necessary wisdom for my growth! Had I not found insight into the challenges of my current relationship, I know my life would have taken a different path, possibly one of great sorrow. I would have continued reliving the guilt and the uncontrollable urge to care for David, constantly mothering him.

I managed to finally leave David, after picking an appropriate time for my growth and his. Now, at sixty-seven years of age, I reflect with gratitude at finding that inconspicuous old business card tacked up on the bulletin board so many years ago. It changed my life, and I will be forever grateful.

Heather Bruce-Bening

ECHOES OF LEMURIA

*T*hroughout my adult life and as far back into childhood as I can remember, I have had a recurring, vivid dream of living under the sea. The dream is always the same; I am a fully functioning, air-breathing being, but I live underwater, experiencing the beauty and fragility of the water world surrounding me. I feel human, but when I look at my body, I am a dolphin. Sadness overwhelms me upon awakening, as though a part of me has been left behind in the dream.

As a student of past life regression, I was required to undergo hypnosis as part of my training. During my first hypnotic session, I recovered the meaning behind my recurring dream of living underwater.

As we begin the regression, I close my eyes and the soft rays of dawn's light filters over crystalline shores, while waves of turquoise water laps at the pale sand. Flowers, luminescent and fragrant, bloom along the water's edge and their petals glow gently as the sun crests the horizon. Swirling mist rises above the ocean's surface and veils the emerald cliffs and the ancient, spiral towers in the distance.

I stand at the boundary between land and sea, feeling the cool grains of sand beneath my bare feet and the gentle pulse of the ocean calling out to me. The air shimmers with the energy of Lemuria. I can sense the song of creatures both seen and unseen. Shadows of dolphins' dance beneath the translucent waves, beckoning me with their joyful presence.

The elders gather nearby, their opalescent robes trailing like liquid silver through the sand. Their eyes reflect the infinite blue of the sea. As the sun climbs higher casting iridescent patterns across the water, they speak in soft, melodic tones, their voices mingling with the peacefulness of the surf.

The elders arrange themselves in a circle around a deep pool ringed with luminous stones that glimmer in the morning sun. The pool's surface stirs, revealing shifting images of the sea and sky entwined.

The sand grows warm, and I feel the waves pulling at my feet as the tide rolls out, leaving behind shells that hum with hidden power. Elder Kaelan, tall and graceful, approaches me with a knowing smile, his hands cradling a shell that glows with inner light.

"The time has come for you to remember." His words echo in my mind and ears as I'm led away to join the circle by the deep pool.

Kneeling beside the pool, I gaze into its depths, feeling the memory of water stir within my bones. The elders begin to chant, their voices weaving a tapestry of sound that vibrates through the earth. My reflection shimmers and elongates as the boundary between my human form and something otherworldly softens.

I step into the pool, and the water rises in a delicate stream, wrapping around my limbs higher and higher until it touches my chin. The light refracts and my skin tingles with the sensation of change. The song of dolphins grows louder, echoing inside my chest.

My arms lengthen and reshape, my fingers fusing into graceful fins. My breath is caught in my throat before shifting and adapting to the new rhythm of the sea. For a heartbeat, I hover between worlds, suspended in a moment of crystalline clarity. Then I slip beneath the surface.

All my senses alight with wonder. Beneath the waves, shafts of sunlight pierce the blue water, illuminating schools of brilliant fish and spiraling columns of coral. I dart through the currents, the world opening before me in vibrant color and sound. Dolphins leap and spin around me, their laughter reverberating in the water. They welcome me with exuberant calls, and together we soar and dive, weaving patterns through the kelp forests and swirling eddies. Joy surges within me and the boundless freedom of the ocean is now my own.

Floating near the surface, I gazed back at the land where my journey began. In that ancient, lost world, I discovered the truth: I am a shapeshifter, kin to both land and sea.

As noon approaches, the ocean's surface glimmers with bright sunshine and the distant shore of Lemuria stirs within me a legacy, a memory carried on every wave, beckoning me back to my terrestrial home.

Standing on terra firma, I feel the hardness of the stone path beneath my feet, undeniably distinct from the sea. I am fully restored to human form, filled with a sense of wonder at the miracle of transformation and the experience of being human once again.

With the back of my hand, I wipe the saltwater from my forehead as the summer breeze caresses the droplets on my skin, creating a chill despite the mid-day warmth. I inhale deeply, savoring the sweet scent of lilies, jasmine, and gardenias blooming in the Gateway Garden, magically transforming the air into a refreshing and delightful atmosphere.

Gazing down, I marvel at the fresh saltwater gathering around my feet. I watch as it spreads onto the massive basalt stones, quickly dissipating in the summer heat. I study the rich detail in the gray and black stones, how the fine-grained crystalline matrix supports the large pieces of crystal.

The massive stones, all laid in perfect symmetry, create a wide and well-worn path leading to the temple. Ancient baobab trees with thick, bottle-shaped trunks and finger-like leaves cast vertical shadows on the stone pathway as the sun reaches its apex. Reflexively, I touch the amethyst talisman hanging by a golden chain around my neck and begin my daily sojourn to the temple.

I hear the patter of feet on the stones and turn to find my family, friends, and neighbors, the people of Lemuria, close behind. Their bodies are slender and graceful, and their limbs are long and strong as they stride with a natural elegance, exhibiting a fluidity of movement.

We greet each other in hushed voices and subdued excitement as we ascend the stone steps and enter the cool, dimly lit gallery of the temple, leaving behind the brilliance of the sun and the deep azure sky.

In remembering my Lemurian lifetime, I know my soul's journey is unique, shaped and designed by the lessons it has chosen for my own growth and evolution in this lifetime. Sometimes I forget what I carry from my previous lifetimes, but this life is my new canvas, and I will paint it with the wisdom I carry, both remembered and not yet achieved.

The challenges I now face are not a punishment, but an invitation to grow. Even though the journey ahead remains uncertain, I know I am guided by the echoes of Lemuria and that my soul's path, unique and luminous, is mine to walk.

Pamela D. Nance

CARRIED BY STONE AND SHADOW

The rock beneath me pulsed—steady, certain. A spiraling force, unseen but unmistakable, rose through the earth and into my body, like breath made of stone. I was sitting beside Te Pito Kura, the sacred navel of the world, on Rapa Nui. The ocean nearby exhaled in rhythm, as if matching the current I felt rising through the volcanic land.

The ground vibrated gently, a subtle resonance that carried memory through the soles of my feet. My hand hovered over the sacred stone. I didn't touch it, not yet. Something in me asked for pause. My eyes closed. My breath slowed.

There was no sound—only the thick, textured silence of presence. The spiral wasn't something I could see. It was something I felt.

It moved through me like water winding through rock. A circling current turned everything inward. The air around me stilled. Time thinned. I slipped into the space between moments, between memory and knowing.

I was not alone.

No voice called out, no shape appeared. But the presence was undeniable. It surrounded me. It was in the stone, in the heat of the sun, in the salt rising from the sea. The Moai stood nearby, tall and grounded, not as guardians but as witnesses. I felt their gaze like a mirror, not of my body—but of my essence.

Then came the shift. A knowing unfolded inside me like light rising behind a mountain ridge. This land knew me. And I knew it.

It wasn't a memory with scenes or names. Just warmth flooding my chest, a tingling in my skin, and the sense that I had crossed this threshold long before. In that moment, I felt a thread of remembrance that stretched not only through Earth's ages—but far beyond. Something in me recalled a pulse that had echoed in other lifetimes... even among the stars.

Tears rose from a place beneath language. I stayed still, allowing the spiral to move freely through me, allowing the presence to hold me. The world fell away. For a moment, I wasn't the visitor. I was the stone. The current. The land. And something more.

Later that day, still carried by that presence, I walked a quiet path along the cliffs. The sea breathed below me, deep and blue and endless. Gulls circled above, their cries distant, as if echoing across centuries. I didn't know where I was going, only that something ahead was waiting.

I came to the opening of Ana Kai Tangata—the ancient cave. Its mouth yawned wide and low, like an invitation and a warning at once. I stood at the threshold, heart pulsing. My body moved forward before my mind could intervene.

Crossing into shadow, the temperature dropped. The world outside dimmed behind me. The air inside carried salt, smoke, and the weight of silence. My feet touched smooth volcanic stone, worn by centuries of waves and reverence.

Light filtered in through jagged breaks above, falling in broken lines across the cave's skin. I reached out and touched the wall—petroglyphs, etched by ancestors whose names had dissolved, yet whose messages endured. Symbols pressed into stone like prayers still vibrating through time.

The cave breathed.

Stillness grew dense. Not absence, but fullness.

And then, something entered. Or perhaps it had been there all along, waiting for me to notice. A presence filled the space. It didn't announce itself. It didn't demand attention. It simply was.

Immense. Steady. Vast.

The air shifted. My breath wasn't mine anymore. It moved through me, part of the cave, part of the pulse I'd felt earlier at Te Pito Kura. My chest expanded, then softened. My awareness opened beyond form.

The presence saw me. Not as I appeared, but as I am—beyond personality, beyond even this lifetime.

And in its presence, I saw myself.

Not the woman who had flown across oceans to reach this island, but something older. A soul shaped by elements and lifetimes. A being woven from star matter and stone.

There was no vision. No flash of history. Only quiet, complete recognition.

I had been here.

And not only here.

The cave didn't offer answers. It offered remembrance. Earthbound and galactic, present and eternal.

Time dissolved. My body softened into stillness. I became the pause between waves. The echo inside stone. The awareness that simply is.

Eventually, the presence settled—still within me but no longer separate. My breath returned to its natural rhythm. I walked slowly back toward the light.

Outside, the sun hung low. The wind touched my skin like an old friend. My hand rested over my chest. The spiral still moved—not from the land this time, but from within.

Rapa Nui had given me two sacred mirrors: the stone and the shadow. The Moai and the cave. One anchored me to the pulse of the earth. The other invited me inward, into the realms beyond time and body.

Together, they awakened something that had been resting for lifetimes. A remembrance, not as story, but as truth. A doorway into who I was—into what I've always been.

I carry it now. That pulse. That stillness. That knowing.

And when I sit quietly—when the breath deepens and the stars begin to shimmer—I return. Not only to the island, but to the cosmic thread it helped me remember.

Hellevi E. Woodman

THE KALEIDOSCOPE OF SOUL'S SPIRAL PATH

The trip had taken twice as long as had been expected. We'd encountered a powerful storm on our way up the steep mountain in the heart of Colombia. Thunder had clapped down on our heads as we rode up the craggy peaks; huge lightning bolts sizzled all around us as heavy rain sent huge hunks of hail hurtling down, completely soaking our clothing. My horse was adept at navigating the boulders, but we were right on the cliff's edge and the storm had made the path a treacherous river of mud.

Every time I glanced down into the deep ravine below, it sent waves of fear coursing through my body. I felt certain that I was going to die and that none of my loved ones at home would ever know what had become of me. I started praying aloud to God and the angels for mercy. Alicia, a Mayan priestess from Guatemala, was on the horse behind me and started to accompany my fervent prayers in Spanish.

Maybe it was the combination of prayers that made the storm finally move past us just as we reached the summit.

I gently slid down from the horse, with the assistance of our guide. It was a relief to have my feet on solid ground.

There was a mystical aura present… the dirt was a beautiful rust-brown and the trees and bushes were a variety of vivid, glowing greens.

Everything felt so alive. A sparkling, crystal creek beckoned me with a deep calling to drink from its life force… to become one with its vibrant flow. I automatically took off my shoes and stepped into the moving water. The cool wetness on the soles of my feet was exhilarating.

Suddenly, a magical mist of euphoria descended upon me. The light was especially beautiful as the late afternoon sun dappled through the tree leaves. As I walked over to the rocky cliff to gaze out over the vast expanse below, a remembrance and a knowing came over me. Gradually, my heart quickened as the realization came into full consciousness.

Oh, my God! This was the place! This was the scene of an incredibly potent vision-experience I had had thirty-eight years previously.

My mind softly reverted back to the memory of that experience. It was 1974 and I was a college student. I had sustained a tumultuous, traumatic breakup from the love of my life and had spent six dreary, gray months in a fog of depression. I busied myself with school and the two part time jobs I worked to make ends meet. My primary employment was in a hospital lab as a phlebotomist. The hours of work always passed quickly as I moved around the hospital, drawing blood samples from diverse types of patients.

I befriended my coworkers, most of whom were also young and just starting out on a life path. A new young man had recently joined our team. He was a work-study student from Antioch College in Ohio and was there to get firsthand experience within the healthcare field.

Steve was different from most people I had encountered before. He was from the East Coast, while I was a native Californian. He was silly and loved to make me laugh. I was serious, especially since my recent heartbreak.

At first, I felt annoyed by his silliness, but I gradually came to appreciate it. I found the joy of laughter to be a healing salve for my broken heart. We slowly began to spend time together outside of work…. A cup of coffee in the morning or a nightcap at a bar after work. He playfully stole our first kiss when we were alone in the hospital elevator.

As it turned out, the universe had provided just the right man, a true "earth angel" to help me heal my love wounds. Gradually, I felt myself learning to trust again as I allowed myself to move forward into a relationship again.

He lived in a wonderful old Victorian house that had been divided into apartments. His was a large room on the second floor with its own bathroom. He had a small porch that he never used, preferring to open the tall windows that stood over the roof covering the main front porch downstairs. We would open those windows and climb out onto the roof below to watch the starry night. It was quite romantic, as we told each other stories or read aloud from a favorite novel or book of poetry by candlelight.

It was in the space of this dreamy cave that we first made love. That was when the vision happened. As we passionately embraced each other, becoming one for the first time, I was transported up, out, and away to another time, another land, another life. The experience was intense, very real, and it filled each of my senses.

We were standing at the precipice of a mountain together, surrounded by a community of elders. We wore long, flowing white robes, as did all those around us and we were in the middle of a sacred ceremony. I was unsure as to exactly what was going on, but was aware that it was magical, mystical, and important. Slowly, the experience faded as I found myself back in the present, clinging to him with an open heart, profoundly transformed.

Now here I was, decades later, standing on that dream-like mountain. Although Steve was not present with me physically, I had been very aware of his spirit's presence on this journey. He had passed, transitioning into spirit nineteen years earlier.

While he was no longer in a physical body, I was. And this was real... very real.

The year after my vision, we had traveled to Colombia. Steve had spent time in Colombia prior to our meeting, and it was a special place for him. He had read and heard about the Kogi indigenous tribe, who had hidden in the mountains and managed to evade all contact with Europeans or any Western influence. He had been on a mission to meet the Kogi people during our trip in 1975. We had traveled to Santa Marta on the coast, at the foot of the Sierra Nevada Mountains, for just that reason.

The Colombians in the city laughed at us, telling us that the Kogi never came down the mountain, and that we would die trying to reach their village at the top of the mountain.

We decided to rethink our plan. But that very afternoon, we were shocked to have three members of the Kogi tribe approach us. We all sat down together and spent hours communicating via hand gestures, body language, and energetic intent. The Kogi did not speak Spanish, and we did not speak their indigenous language.

They shared their coca leaves with us; Steve shared his toothpaste with them, showing them how the calcium it contained could help to release the active ingredient of the coca leaf. The lack of verbal communication did not prevent true connection. We spent the afternoon laughing, sharing, and enjoying each other's company. We also took pictures together.

The vision-experience, so many years ago, I thought to myself… and then it all started to make sense.

My vision had been a glimpse into another lifetime, a time we had shared long ago. That explained why I had been so drawn to journey back to Colombia, after receiving an email newsletter announcing, "Dawn of a New Time." As soon as I opened the email and started to read, I felt my chest expand wide open as my heart filled with love and anticipation.

There was a picture of several Kogi in the email, which triggered a memory of 1975 and the pictures we had taken. I ran to the garage and found the pictures…. Yes! The same dress, the same tribe! I immediately knew that this gathering was something I had to attend.

For the very first time, the four tribes of the Sierra Nevada would open their village to Westerners. Spirit was telling them that it was time, that the very future of our Earth depended upon it. They were asked to share the traditional ways of living in reciprocity with the Earth, if our planet was to survive.

In 2011 I traveled to Colombia for the ten-day event. I was alone, but Steve was with me in spirit. There were 130 people who gathered from twenty-five countries. Our days were full of ceremony and teachings from indigenous elders from around the globe. We learned about growing and harvesting food and educating children. We heard about their spiritual belief and the system of reciprocity with Mother Earth.

I returned for a smaller event the following year, in 2012. This time, there were only thirty-five others in attendance. It had been decided that we would be allowed to travel to the most sacred part of their land, on top of the mountain. This was when I rode on horseback through thunder, lightning, and hail, to arrive right at the place of my vision-experience. This journey ignited my remembering.

These experiences, along with others, have provided a weaving of remembrance. They have allowed me to fit together puzzle pieces that provide a picture of the spiral of my soul's path. Perhaps time is non-linear and is a spiral.

I believe I lived in a previous time and culture that provides insight into pertinent knowledge we need today. I now realize that part of my current life's mission is to remember those lessons: trusting and living in sync with Spirit and facilitating others' remembrance of personal Divine life paths in reciprocity for all.

Susan Melnikow

SOUL'S INHERITANCE

*E*arly one morning my neighbor exclaims, "Martin is crazy! This is getting out of hand!"

Agitated, with a frazzled voice and a distressed look, she continues. "How much longer does this have to go on? He is so rude! He bumps into us without even apologizing, walks by without saying hello. His wife walks on the other side of the street while he is on this side. His children are never seen talking to him. How does he possibly drive if he can't see people while walking?"

I am listening in silence while an emotional avalanche of anger and frustration pours out of Anna. It appears that, again today, Martin has bumped into one of the neighbors without saying hello or sorry and has continued walking without acknowledging what took place.

After I say goodbye to Anna, I walk away with a burden. This is an enigma requiring a resolution. *This is not my riddle*, I am thinking, so why am I so eager to solve it? It is Martin's family dilemma, not mine. He is a neighbor.

Then my mind begins playing a rewind slide show about all the issues we had with Martin as a neighbor throughout the years. If I go and knock on every neighbor's door, each one, without exception, will share some similar outraged concern. None of them will have a kind word to say about Martin.

Why is he so alienated from the rest of the world? Why is he not concerned enough to show civil and respectful behavior and be considerate to people that surround him, his family and neighbors? He does not have any friends. That's understandable. Who would want to be friends with someone who intentionally avoids courtesy, ignores greetings, never offers a kindness, or speaks considerately?

By education, Martin is an engineer, but he chooses not to practice his expertise. During the daytime, Martin can be seen going through the stuff in his cluttered garage. No one knows what he does in there for hours, day after day after day.

I continue to be preoccupied with Martin. "He doesn't even have a job! Martin's wife's family is the sole provider for their household. What kind of father is he to their five children when he can't fulfill his duties as a parent? His eldest child is troubled with addictions and violent behavior and was unable to graduate from high school. His other kids are battling to navigate their own challenging issues. His kids are lacking a guide who can help them because their mother faces severe anxiety," I vent aloud.

A strong voice from the back of my head speaks to me: *You can resolve this if you begin praying for him.*

I stop and an assured feeling from my invisible past envelopes me with a declaration: *Yes, you can do this, you know how to do this. You do have a solution for this.*

What is this wisdom and where is it coming from?

This internal knowledge flows like a breeze of confidence and warmth into my heart, almost like a renewed passion for riding a bike that has gone untouched for many years.

I surrender to the voice I trust. I begin mapping my steps of action by recalling my memory of what to do.

I need to commit to a prayer for Martin and his family and to completely stop any negative thoughts or observations, no matter what he does and how his actions make me feel.

It will be a daily, simple prayer, visualizing him happily holding hands with family and smiling. In my prayer scene, I hear neighbors' surprised comments about his miraculous change. And all is well in that scene.

Why do I feel so comfortable with this "knowing"?

Content in my heart, I go home and begin my prayers for Martin and his family by visualizing the same scene where all is well for all.

Days pass by, then months. Nothing has changed yet. I persist in my prayers. There is no doubt in my heart and mind that this is going to work. How do I know this? Where is my assurance coming from?

One evening I am watching an interview about ancient Egypt that explains how priestesses performed their ceremonies and meditations in the ancient temples. On the screen is a picture of how the ancient priestesses may have looked. My eyes are glued to that picture. I stop, take a screenshot and stare… Chills roll down my back as a recollection of something strongly familiar takes over me. I was *there*, and I was part of the prayer ceremony. No one to ask but my heart.

That night I go to bed feeling as if I am in front of a door that is closed by memory, yet I'm aware of what's behind it.

The next morning, I wake up feeling stronger, knowing with more certainty that I was there in Egypt as a priestess. Then I remember my presence in other parts of the world practicing the same skill, praying for the wellness of all and offering healing with herbs.

Weeks pass. I continue praying for Martin and his family. One Sunday morning when I open my car trunk to retrieve a bag, I hear "Good morning, Ida, how are you?"

I turn back and see my neighbor Martin looking at me. Is this real? He said good morning! He actually knows my name.

I greet him back with a warm smile and thank the infinite spirit for hearing my prayers.

Martin walks away like nothing different took place. More days pass. My neighbors are gathered and share their shocking experiences of Martin greeting them and making eye contact or helping them with something they needed to take care of. They can't understand what caused the shift.

Another day, from my window, I see Martin and his wife walking together, holding each other's hands, smiling, heading to the car. Infinite spirit receives a big thank you from my heart for helping Martin.

Neighbors keep noticing more changes and sharing the miraculous transformation, struggling to connect the dots. What do we owe this? I continue my prayers. The shift began after six months of my commitment.

Month after month, Martin and his family are getting closer to each other and we all witness and rejoice in the positive turn.

My experience in another life nudged me to use what I know and reach to the invisible helping hand of the universe. The memory of knowing gives me the strength to apply my skills. A carving on the gemstone of my heart is reactivated, and I rejoice.

The mystery remains unrevealed. This awakened gift is a portal to log into the network of our Source, with benefit for all.

Ida Ra Nalbandian

RETURN TO PHILAE

My first trip to Egypt happened during the COVID pandemic, when much of the world was still locked down and moving through uncertainty. Traveling at that time wasn't easy, but I didn't feel I really had a choice. My decision came through a dream—one of those rare ones that feel more real than waking life.

In the dream, I was standing inside the Great Pyramid. It was quiet, still, almost like the air was charged with something. The Goddess Hathor appeared and gave me a blessing. Standing next to me was Anubis. He wasn't threatening; he felt protective, like an old friend. He was there to help raise my energy, like tuning it into a frequency I didn't even know existed. When I woke up, I knew I had to go to Egypt. I didn't need to ask why. The dream gave me a clear direction.

That trip changed something deep inside me, but the most powerful part of it didn't happen until the very end at the Temple of Isis.

On the morning we left Luxor for Aswan, I woke up around five a.m. My guide, Mohammed, and I went to the train station. It was a quiet morning, the kind where time feels stretched out. We stood on the platform waiting, and every time a train came, Mohammed would say, "Not this one." Then another train would pass. "Still not this one."

I started feeling nervous. This was one of my last days in Egypt and I knew how important the temple was for me. Years before, a medium told me I'd lived two past lives connected to the Temple of Isis. I had always felt drawn to it—like a thread pulling me toward something unfinished.

Our train finally arrived—four hours late. It didn't even take us all the way to Aswan. We had to jump off and grab a local ricksha. Everything on the trip suddenly felt rushed and unpredictable. But somehow, I remained calm. I knew I had to get to that temple, no matter what.

When we finally reached the dock and sat in the boat that would take us across the water to Philae Island, something shifted in me. I started crying. Not sobbing, not overwhelmed, just quiet, steady tears. The closer we got to the island, the more I felt like I was returning somewhere I had once known very well. It didn't feel like visiting a historical site. It felt like going home.

As we approached, I told Mohammed I didn't want him to tell me anything about the place yet. I needed to explore it on my own first.

When we arrived, I stepped onto the island and bent down to kiss the ground. It wasn't planned. It just felt natural. I greeted the earth, asked silently for permission to enter, and thanked whatever was still alive there.

Without really thinking, I walked straight toward a set of stone windows that look out onto the Nile. My tears came harder. I cried in a way I hadn't in a long time—and I didn't care who saw me. It wasn't sadness exactly. It was more like something old was being released.

At that moment, I also started bleeding. It wasn't expected. It wasn't the time for it. But I took it as a sign that my body was in sync with what was happening. I was giving something back to the land, to the river, to the temple.

I walked through the temple slowly, not really thinking, just feeling. A deep sense of loneliness rose up in me, not the kind you feel in a crowd, but something older, like a memory. I suddenly knew, without needing proof, that I had once been here—not in this life, but before. I had been one of the last priestesses walking these halls before the temple was closed down.

That loneliness had followed me in this life, too. Being here made it all make sense. It wasn't just about personal sadness, it was about something ancient, a role I had once played, a connection that had been cut off.

Later I learned, the temple had been officially closed around 550 CE, when Emperor Justinian ordered all the old temples to be shut down. This had been the last active temple of the Egyptian religion. After that, the rituals stopped. The songs, the offerings, the ceremonies were silenced.

But I felt that silence still holding something.

I remembered the stories of how the priestesses used to walk to the river to mourn Osiris, to offer their tears. It wasn't just grief; it was a sacred act. They kept the cycle of life, death, and rebirth alive through those offerings. They held the flame of love, of union between spirit and body.

Returning to that place felt like a reminder that we are both physical and spiritual beings. That our job—then and now—is to remember that we are the beloved and to carry that remembrance back into the world.

We aren't separate from these ancient stories. We are living them again in new ways.

As I walked out of the temple, I didn't feel finished. I felt reconnected. The place didn't give me answers. It gave me a remembering. And that was enough.

Annette Assmy

SOULS REUNITE

a close friend and I talked about all things spiritual, endlessly and obsessively. But when we started discussing past lives, suddenly we both decided to stop because we suspected we had shared at least one past life.

Curious to confirm our intuition, we devised an experiment: Over a single weekend, from our separate residences, we would each conduct a past life regression to see if we had indeed shared a past life. If so, there would be noticeable similarities in our experiences.

Both of us were both experienced meditators and proficient in automatic writing. The methodology we followed was simple: Independently, we would each enter a meditative trance, asking to remember a past life we had lived together that held significant meaning for our spiritual connection. We would request as much specific information as possible, details we could compare, validate, and understand.

During our meditation, as visions and insights surfaced, we'd record everything that came through by writing it out longhand, filling pages upon pages of paper with what we received.

When I entered my regression, I immediately found myself in South Africa. I was a white South African barrister, and my friend was my business partner and closest companion. While I did a great deal of good for people through my work as a lawyer in that life, I held racist beliefs, and I must have made enemies, because I was killed in a violent uprising in the region. My death was brutal, but as I reviewed it, I felt at peace. It seemed like retribution for the inequalities I had perpetuated in that lifetime.

Throughout this life, I have lived in various places, often choosing integrated areas where I feel comfortable. It is important to me that I live alongside people of different racial and cultural backgrounds, in peace and harmony. This has become a theme in my life. I believe I am working through the karma of my past life in South Africa, where racial disparities were prevalent in my culture.

My friend also completed a self-regression, and when we compared our notes, we were both astonished, continually experiencing chills as we discovered the uncanny similarities between our accounts. We had both focused on a life in South Africa, even though neither of us had ever discussed being connected to that country before.

In that past life, we had been best friends, white men, and business partners. Our notes aligned perfectly. In that life, we both agreed, my friend was married to a younger woman, but their relationship was fraught with difficulty. Ultimately, in this past life, he killed her, and their house burned down, although he survived.

My friend and I both realized that the woman he had been involved with in South Africa had also played a role in an earlier stage of his current life. I saw that the woman who perished in the fire was someone he had dated in this lifetime. They had been intensely drawn to each other but had an equally turbulent relationship. There had even been a fire in the house they shared, shortly before their separation.

But in this lifetime, my friend was able to leave, angrily but without violence. We both felt that he had resolved much of his karma with her. Neither of them had physically harmed the other, unlike what happened in their previous incarnation.

In our current lives, my friend and I remain close, but with no trace of romance between us. A hallmark of our past life was the joy we found in storytelling—sitting together, laughing and discussing all manner of things. Interestingly, this dynamic persists in our present friendship.

When we compared our separate notes, we were amazed to discover that the period we had both focused on was within two years of each other in the late 1800s. Moreover, it took place in a country and on a continent where neither of us had a present-day connection. Our notes seamlessly interwove, confirming and expanding upon each other's experiences.

Ultimately, my friend and I wholeheartedly believe we have shared a number of past lives. We have made a pact that at the right time, under the right circumstances, in another dimension of time and space, we will find each other again. Our souls will continue sharing laughter, friendship, and light, as we always have.

Barbara Ross Greaney

A TERRIFYING VISION

*Y*ears ago, my husband Gary and I went on an organized trip to sacred sites in Scotland. After visiting stone circles, standing stones, medieval churches, and an enchanted forest on the Scottish mainland, we slowly made our way to the sacred Isle of Iona, which is called "the cradle of Celtic Christianity in Scotland."

To reach Iona, we undertook an arduous, day long journey. First, we had to get to Oban, on the west coast of the mainland, and take a ferry to the Isle of Mull. Then we took a bus across Mull and another ferry across the mile-wide Sound of Iona. At last, we reached our destination: a tiny island, only three miles long by one-and-a-half miles wide.

Perhaps because it had taken so much effort to get to Iona, the place immediately felt special. It was a peaceful place, a holy place that had been a destination for pilgrims for nearly 1,500 years, ever since St. Columba and his group of twelve monks established a monastery there in 563 AD.

There was something "in the air" in Iona, as if more were happening than my five senses could identify.

That evening, Gary and I wandered over to the nearby 12th-century stone chapel and sat quietly, absorbing the ambience of the place, sensing the energy of prayer and devotion that had soaked into the ancient stone walls for nearly a thousand years. We sang a simple chant, and oddly enough, it sounded like there was a choir accompanying us. I turned around to see who had joined us, but no one was there.

During the next two days, Marga, our tour guide, led us to the most important sites. We walked around the famous abbey and marveled at the medieval nunnery and an intricately carved high cross. Nearby was St. Oran's graveyard, where as many as forty-eight medieval monks, clan chiefs, and Scottish kings were buried—including the rumored remains of the 12th-century Macbeth, on whom Shakespeare based his tale.

Finally, Marga led us up a steep, stony trail to the highest point on Iona, Dun I. The hill rises 333 feet above sea level. At the top is a cairn, all that remains of an Iron Age hillfort. The panoramic view was magnificent, but we hadn't hiked all that way for the view. We had come to visit Tobar nah Aoise, also known as the Well of Eternal Youth, the Well of Healing, and the Well of St. Brigid, named after the 5th-century Irish saint who is patroness of Ireland.

Legend says that St. Brigid blessed the waters of the well on a visit to Iona on the summer solstice. St. Brigid is closely linked to the Celtic sun-goddess Brigid, who was worshipped throughout Ireland and Scotland for millennia, before Christianity began supplanting pagan ways. The story of St. Brigid's blessing the well on the summer solstice, an important holiday in the pagan calendar, strongly suggested that the well had been holy in pre-Christian times.

To find St. Brigid's Well, we walked down the slope toward a cleft in the rocks. The well is a natural, perhaps spring-fed pool in the shape of a heart, nestled against a large granite outcrop. Visitors often touch or drink the water, but Marga had something else in mind. We sat on the ground next to the well and wove Brigid's crosses out of reeds. The arms of these crosses are slightly off-center, resembling an ancient sun symbol as much as a Christian cross. Bending and weaving the slender, flexible reeds together felt like a sacred task.

Marga led us in a brief song dedicated to Brigid and told us to make a wish, or set an intention, and place our reed crosses in the water. We did so silently, and then we each found a comfortable place to sit and meditate.

I walked a short distance away from the group, close to where the ground sharply dropped away, and sat down on a patchy bit of grass. I faced the holy well, rather than the drop-off behind me. Puffy clouds drifted across the blue sky, and in the distance, the wake of a ferry cut like an arrow through the water. A gentle breeze ruffled my hair. I closed my eyes and sank into a deep meditation.

As if in a vision, I saw myself performing a ritual act, placing a Brigid's cross in the still waters of the pond. I knew that worshipping the Goddess was forbidden, but I felt safe here, at this ancient holy well, far from the settlement below.

Suddenly, a group of five soldiers rushed out from the boulders behind the pool. Swords raised, they ran toward me screaming. Before I knew what was happening, they picked me up and tossed me over the edge of the hill! I was falling, falling—arms splayed out in freefall—I knew I would soon smash onto the rocks below and shatter into smithereens.

Adrenalin pumping through my system, I snapped out of the vision just before I would have crashed onto the ground. Trembling with terror, I looked around. I was still sitting on the patchy bit of grass near the edge of the hill. Puffy clouds still drifted across the blue sky, and in the distance, the wake of a ferry cut like an arrow through the water. A gentle breeze ruffled my hair.

There were no soldiers. I wasn't lying broken and bleeding on the rocks far below. I pinched my arms, just to be sure. Ouch! Yes, I was still alive.

I tried to understand what had happened. My vision had been so vivid, so real. I had been picked up and tossed like a rag doll to my death. It had happened!

Suddenly, I realized that I'd had a spontaneous past life experience, a vision that showed me the horrifying death that, unknown to me, had haunted my present life.

I had always been irrationally afraid of standing on the side of a hill or cliff with a sharp drop below. I didn't mind flying in airplanes or other kinds of heights, but falling off a cliff terrified me.

Now I knew why. Embedded deep within me was the memory of that excruciating death.

I remembered reading that sometimes, when we learn about a traumatic past life experience, we are freed of the trauma. Perhaps Brigid's Well was offering me that opportunity.

Elyn Aviva

NUMBING GRIEF

*Y*ears ago, when we moved to our five-acre property in rural Oregon, we dreamed of creating a nature sanctuary in harmony with the land. We planned to take the time to listen and feel the shimmers in the wind, notice a sudden hush or stillness, and be conscious of other signals from the land as we developed it.

However, an injury slowed us down. I was in a cast, only able to gaze longingly outside at the giant fir trees, native shrubs, and visiting deer. My task was to be patient and accept this gap as I waited to heal. This project had been incubating for years, so the wait was a challenging experience for me.

During this gap time, a vivid dream profoundly touched me and opened the path for me. In my dream, an old Native American woman leaned over a broken ceramic bowl on the ground before her. Tears ran down her wrinkled brown face, and her hands shook as she reached out tenderly to touch the fragments of the bowl. I could sense her memories and feelings. I knew she had lovingly shaped the clay bowl from the red earth and painted the bowl with age-old, sacred earth designs.

Why am I witnessing this?

Suddenly, I realized that I was the old woman. I was inhabiting her being as my own. As I rocked back and forth, I felt her deep wails rising up from my own belly.

I realized that, in a former life, I had been the caretaker of this sacred bowl for my tribe, which had always lived in a covenant with the Earth Spirit. It was the context we lived in, like fish in water. All our actions, decisions, plans, and knowledge sprang from this relationship with the Earth. In return, the Earth and the energies of nature gave us comfort, security, and wisdom. Living in this way has brought us harmony and balance for generations.

And now, this broken bowl on the ground before me was the final signal that the old ways were gone. The tribe was disintegrating, and our pact with the Earth had been broken. All my life, I have created offerings for this bowl, honoring the sacredness of our relationship with the Earth. Now the reality of our tribal prophecy about this time was upon us.

I was overcome by a grief almost too deep to bear, engulfed in numbing despair.

Suddenly, I heard words expressing hope. *These times are different. People are coming back together as caretakers for the Earth. The sacred bowl of life is filling again. A new cycle is beginning.*

At that moment, I understood that this ancient grief from another lifetime had impeded my ability to cultivate an intimate relationship with our land. Perhaps my recent injury manifested as an unconscious block, uncovering a deep, numbing grief about the loss of partnership with the Earth.

But I knew from these hopeful words that it was time to acknowledge my grief, move forward, and open my heart once again. I was ready to begin dwelling in the land, not just on it, feeling her rhythms, sensing her daily messages, feeling her support.

I saw, in my mind's eye, that people are gathering again. A quickening and an awakening are stirring hearts throughout the world. People are feeling called to be caretakers of the sacred bowl of life and to reverently care for life in their own bodies, other beings, and Earth herself.

The dream gave me hope and a tremendous clearing. This message helped me understand that holding onto grief had hindered my connection with the land, and I was now able to move forward.

Ann Marie Holmes

TWO LIVES, ONE SOUL

uring my most recent past life regression, I was taken through two vastly different lifetimes. Though these lives were not directly connected by time, place, or identity, they revealed to me the profound duality of existence—two opposing, yet complementary, expressions of the human experience.

I was no more than six years old—a quiet, wide-eyed Native American girl living on a vast prairie that stretched endlessly beneath the open sky. My earliest memory in that life is of sitting at a rough-hewn wooden table outside, its grain worn smooth by sun, rain, and the steady passage of time. I was surrounded by my family—or what remained of it.

At the head of the table sat my father. An Englishman by birth, he held himself with a rigid composure, a man once softened by love but now distant and hardened by grief. My siblings sat in silence, as still as strangers, shaped by our father's quiet resentment. And beside me was an empty seat. That was where my mother should have been—if she had survived.

But she had died giving birth to me.

Her absence haunted him, and I was the living reminder of his loss. To him, and to the rest of my family, I was the reason she was no longer with us.

They never said it aloud, but the weight of their silence and the distance in their eyes spoke for them. I was the unwanted reminder of her absence.

Meals were quiet and mechanical. We didn't speak, didn't share stories or laughter. We ate not out of joy or tradition, but simply to survive. I was there, but not part of them. I was a ghost in my own family, the unwanted memory of a woman they all loved more than they could ever love me.

Loneliness became my companion.

With no warmth from my family, I turned to the prairie itself. I wandered barefoot in those fields for hours each day, my small feet brushing through wildflowers and soft earth. The wind, the birds, the tall grass that danced in the sun—these were my friends. The trees listened without judgment, and the animals accepted me without question. It was the only place I felt held.

Still, I carried an emptiness inside me. I was a child, but I was burdened by a sorrow too large for my years. My early years were spent tired, unseen, and deeply alone.

One afternoon, as the sun dipped low and painted the river gold, I found myself at the water's edge, skipping rocks while listening to the current whisper its secrets. For a moment, I felt peace, the kind that only the Earth had ever given me. But then, I slipped. My foot caught on the slick edge of a stone, and I fell hard. My head struck a rock and the world went silent.

Death came instantly.

There was no one there to call my name. No one searched for me when the sun set, and I didn't return. My absence was met with the same silence I had known in life.

No one mourned me. No one wept.

But in that still, quiet passing, I finally returned to the place I had always belonged—not to a family that could not love me, but to the prairie that always had. The Earth welcomed me back as its own. And in its silent embrace, I was no longer a ghost.

I was home.

My first memory of the second lifetime came in a sudden, vivid flash—shiny black patent leather shoes tapping gently against a gravel driveway. I was stepping out of the back seat of a sleek, silver car, the sunlight bouncing off its glossy surface. A gloved hand reached out to meet mine—gentle, guiding, familiar. I was ushered into a grand English Tudor home, stately and proud, that sat nestled among carefully manicured hedges and ivy-covered stone.

Inside, life unfolded like a carefully written symphony—elegant, refined, and perfectly orchestrated. The halls echoed with the quiet steps of those who cared for me: attentive nannies, soft-spoken governesses, and dedicated staff who made sure every part of my young life was tended to with precision and love. I was a girl of eight or nine, small in size but already accustomed to a world where comfort and care were a constant.

Though my parents were often away—consumed by social obligations and business affairs—I never felt neglected. Their presence was distant, but the warmth I lacked from them was generously provided by the other adults who raised me. I was doted on, instructed, and gently molded into a young lady of poise and promise.

Each day followed a graceful rhythm. I wore finely tailored dresses crafted from the softest silks and linens. Meals were quiet affairs, prepared by skilled chefs who anticipated my needs before I ever voiced them. My education was private, personal, and immersive. I was tutored in languages, literature, and the arts. Music became my first love—classical piano and voice filled my afternoons. Song was where I expressed what I could not yet put into words.

By the time I reached adolescence, I was already a young woman of refinement. I had been raised not just to exist in society, but to carry it forward with dignity. The expectations were high, but they never felt burdensome. I had been trained for this life, and I moved through it with a deep sense of belonging.

In time, I got married. My husband was a man of character and quiet strength. With him, I found a deeper layer of love—one rooted not just in passion or partnership, but in mutual respect and a shared commitment to building a life of warmth and meaning. Together, we raised children who were the joy of our days. Where there had once been quiet order, now there was family, connection, and the beautiful chaos of love.

Despite the privileges that surrounded me, I felt an undeniable pull to serve beyond the boundaries of our estate. I gave my time and resources freely, helping to organize aid for struggling families and supporting orphanages. I became a quiet force in the lives of those who had no one else. It wasn't about status. It was simply who I had become: a woman who had been given so much and chose to give in return.

The years passed gently, marked by milestones and memories. I watched my children become parents, and my grandchildren bring new life and laughter into our home. The house that had once loomed large in my childhood now felt like an extension of my own soul, filled with the legacy of love we had cultivated within its walls.

When my final days came, I lay surrounded by those I cherished most. Children, grandchildren, lifelong friends, and faithful caregivers stood by my side. The room was warm, filled with flowers and the soft strains of the music I had once played. There was no sadness in that space, only gratitude and peace.

As I took my last breath, it was with a full heart. I had lived a life of grace—not just of comfort, but of connection, compassion, and purpose. I had given the best of myself, and in return, life had given back more than I ever dreamed.

In my current life, I've come to recognize echoes of those past lives in subtle but unmistakable ways. My biological family mirrors the emotional landscape of that first life on the prairie. I was marked by that same quiet ache of invisibility, the sense of being an outsider within my own home.

Yet, just as life carries forward its challenges, it also carries forward its gifts. Over the years, I've drawn to myself a soul family—friends, mentors, and companions who have felt instantly familiar, as if we've known one another far longer than this life could possibly explain. Their presence in my world has been a balm, a reminder of the deep love and unwavering support I once knew in my privileged past lifetime.

In seeing both of these lifetimes reflected in my current journey, I've come to understand that my soul is seeking balance, learning through both absence and abundance, through isolation and connection. In this life, I carry the wisdom of both.

Laura Maher

LOVE AND LOSS

My daughter attended Walford School for her elementary education. We were a tight-knit community characterized by enthusiasm for the Waldorf educational approach as well as love and caring for each other.

There was a boy named Thomas in my daughter's class. From the moment we met, I felt a deeply special connection. I would speak with him whenever the opportunity arose, such as after school events and community gatherings. He, too, enjoyed our connection; he was often excited to share with me the new things he was learning.

One day, as eleven-year-old Thomas was climbing a large tree on his parents' property, the worst came to pass. He fell, landing on his head, and died shortly afterwards. This heartbreaking event was a shock to our entire community; we all grieved and came together to support his family.

Some members of Waldorf communities are part of a spiritual philosophy called *anthroposophy*, within which it is common to hold a three-day vigil with the body of the deceased. This practice can be found in cultures across the globe. The intention is to help the personality with the transition from the physical body into the next dimensions of the spiritual world.

Thomas' parents arranged such a vigil for him and each of us in the community signed up so there would always be someone with him, day and night, over the three days. People who hold vigil for the deceased can spend it however they see fit. They might sit quietly, praying and meditating, or speak freely with the deceased. They can read to them or perhaps play a musical instrument.

I had signed up for the second day of the vigil, from midnight to four a.m. When I entered the vigil room, I saw his body in the casket and felt his expanded awareness literally filling the entire room. It was sad and beautiful at the same time. His awareness was so grand and there was a deep peacefulness about it.

I sat on the couch next to his body and began to speak to him, saying hello and that I was sorry he fell. I told him that I loved him, that I would miss him, and that I wished him well on his new journey.

His parents had placed his favorite books in the room, so I picked one up and began to read it. At once, there was a remarkable shift in his expanded awareness, which immediately began to condense down and became the consciousness, the personality, that I knew and loved as young Thomas. Right then and there, he was sitting next to me on the couch. He was back being Thomas, no longer residing in that expanded awareness. It was almost like he was embodied again.

The experience was beautiful. Tears filled my eyes, and I continued to read books to Thomas while he sat beside me. After a time, he resumed his expanded state, and I sat there quietly for the remainder of my vigil time.

After my vigil with Thomas, I returned home and promptly fell asleep. Within moments, I left my body and found myself astral traveling at a high speed over water. I traveled for a long time. I thought to myself it must be an ocean below me. Eventually, I saw land and, in the distance, a small medieval town on a hillside. I landed in what appeared to be a small vineyard surrounded by an ancient stone wall.

As I looked around the vineyard, I saw a young man standing there. I quickly approached him, noticing his kind face, and said, "Did you know that Thomas died?"

"Yes," he responded. In that instant, I knew that this young man was a prior incarnation of Thomas. He was someone I had known well and loved in that town during my own lifetime then.

I stayed with him for a brief while. No more words were spoken; we simply shared the joy of recognition and reconnection.

More scenes appeared. In one, I found myself standing outside of a tavern of some kind. I was dressed in rags and realized I was a homeless beggar seeking food. Two of the people who eventually emerged from the tavern and gave me food have played important roles in my current personal and professional life, as Paul. In another scene, I was mistreated by a group of four or five adolescents who were having fun harassing and degrading me as a beggar. I felt the anguish of not being seen as a real person. I wanted them to know that I had feelings and desires like theirs, but I could not communicate this to them.

I astral traveled back home, awoke in my bed, and cried about the experiences and the realizations from that lifetime. While the acuteness of the experience ended that morning, over the next two days I found that, both awake and asleep, I maintained a type of dual consciousness: one of me as Paul and one as the former beggar. I was able to shift back and forth, to be both personalities rather easily, to make the change seamlessly.

Eventually, the dual consciousness faded, and I was back to being simply Paul. When the memory of that lifetime receded, I missed it as I'd found a kind of freedom by residing in it.

During those two days of dual consciousness, I wondered if I could identify the medieval town. Where had I lived? I thought I might be able to identify it through research and photographs. Towards that end, I decided to visit my local library and pored for hours through books about medieval towns in Europe.

To my good fortune, I came across a photograph that was similar to the perspective of the image I had in my mind. It was an old black-and-white photo of Assisi, Italy. When I saw the photo, I immediately recognized it, and with that recognition came a surge of emotion. I thought to myself, *I'd like to travel there someday*. I wanted to see what it would be like after my intensive recollections from so long ago.

Two weeks later, I was fortunate to receive an invitation to attend a work-related conference in Sicily, Italy. I enthusiastically accepted and started making travel plans to attend the conference, and of course, to visit Assisi afterwards.

Approximately two months later, after attending the conference, I was on my way north to Assisi. I arrived at midday. As I walked around, I found the town very familiar. I also found that, rather than daytime, I preferred wandering the streets at night, after most people had retired for the evening. I knew those streets and felt comfortable roaming them alone at night.

While there, I was surprised and pleased to find that I could easily return to that experience of dual consciousness. If I chose, I could be the beggar again and see the town through those eyes. Because I also retained my consciousness as Paul, it was not as troubling as it had been in that lifetime. Seeing it through my current eyes allowed the beggar me to appreciate that life for what it had been and what it had offered, including experiences and lessons about cruelty, hope, love, and kindness.

My journeys to Assisi taught me much about my own soul's biography, how our experiences through lifetimes accumulate, and how we learn from those experiences. I realized that we bring those experiences and insights forward into our current lives.

I saw, too, how certain people travel with us from lifetime to lifetime, playing different roles, helping us on our paths.

Paul J. Mills

THE ROMAN GLADIATOR

I had recently been introduced to using the process of hypnotic regression as a tool to tap into the idea of past lives. I was absolutely fascinated. This curiosity became so potent that I did my own research and found a licensed hypnotist who focused his practice in this area.

Imagine my excitement and nervousness as I approached the hypnotist's office door. He answered quickly and yet it also seemed there was enough time for me to turn and go away. *Was I ready to see if this hypnotic regression stuff was legit?* As the handle turned and the door opened, I made the commitment to stay.

What could go wrong? Will I wake up with a headache and no story? I was willing to go for it.

The man with whom I had scheduled this session introduced himself and explained that he had been in engineering until his mother took ill and started talking in fevered states about living other lives. He became engrossed in the idea of past lives and chose to "go down the rabbit hole" wholeheartedly, obtaining a license as a clinical hypnotist. Upon hearing this from him, I became calm internally, knowing I could now trust both him and the process.

As we got into the procedure of regression, I felt my mind slowly and steadily move into territory I was not aware of, never mind familiar with. I admit, it was hard to get my brain to quiet down enough to let the rest of my mind find its voice, so to speak. But we did get to the rhythm, the pulse, the cadence that "set me free" and I started to connect with a storyline just below the surface of my "usual self" story.

The hypnotist asked questions that brought me back to a moment of antiquity. He asked about the surroundings, what I was wearing, if I knew where I was or why I was there. He did not push or prompt but simply asked his questions in a calm voice then waited for my reply. This approach made me very comfortable. I wanted to talk to this person, so I answered his questions.

I was a young boy, maybe six or seven years old, and had very recently arrived at the place I was seeing before me. It was new and loud and busy and crowded and scary because I didn't know anybody here. The people who ran this place were called *Romans*. They were feared and hated because they were warriors who came to a place and either took over everything or destroyed it.

They had come to where my family lived and seized my mother, my sisters, and me. They took all the food and things we had at home. Then they marched through our village doing the same to all the houses and people. But sometimes they just killed people, right in front of us. I don't know why. I am afraid they will kill us, too. Soon, they take my mother and sisters away and take me to where the soldiers camp.

At the camp, I am told to do what the soldiers tell me to do, but I don't know their language, so sometimes they beat me when I don't do what they want. Not all the soldiers are bad, though. A few of the young soldiers are nice to me. They give me extra food and don't hit me. One special soldier seems to pay attention to me. He watches me when I'm working. He is never mean, and he can give orders to other men.

After a few days we leave here and march for days and days. When we get to where they want to go, I'm told, "This is Rome. The greatest place in the world."

What I can tell you is Rome is loud and busy and crowded with different kinds of people everywhere and strange animals, too. The nice soldier, the one who watched me and was not mean, said he was taking me to the place where I would now live. He put me up on his horse so I could ride with him and we went to a place so big, with walls so high, I could not see the top or the end of the walls.

There were many gates into this place. It was confusing, and I was afraid if I got lost there, no one would even know. So I stayed close to the nice soldier. He took me to a part of this place that had a ramp to go from the top, where the sunshine was, to a place carved out below the earth, like a huge cave. Under the ground, there were hundreds of men and horses and weapons. It was very loud and smelly, too.

We rode our horse deep into this underground cavern and then the nice soldier stopped the horse and told me to follow him. We were in a nicer part of this place with chairs and tables and fire light. There was a group of men talking, but they stopped when my soldier entered. One of the men came to my soldier. They made a special sign to each other and then started talking. I could tell it was about me because they kept looking over at me. I was getting scared that my soldier was giving me away to this man who seemed to live in this strange, smelly place.

And that is what happened, but it wasn't horrible like I was afraid it might be. The new man was also a nice man, and he had agreed to take me on as an apprentice in the work he did in this place. My nice soldier had asked this man to take me because we came from places near each other that Rome had conquered.

It got easier after a while for the nice man and me to talk and understand each other. This made me very happy, because I could tell he was happy with me and the work I did. He liked talking with me and we formed a friendship. I was technically his slave, but that was a good thing, because it meant nobody else could take me away or be mean to me. I was glad that if I was going to be a slave, at least the nice soldier had found a nice master for me.

The hypnotist then asked me to "move forward in time." The image that came was of the same location, but I was several years older. I was now an adolescent who was strong and fast and quick on my feet, and I could think for myself, too. All this was because my master really cared about me. He was a man who valued "good character," he would say. He was the one who taught me how to read and permitted me to serve when he had guests visit his quarters.

By sanctioning this, he allowed me to casually observe people and start to understand the games people play when they want something. My master was a man who could "open doors," and nobody wanted to be on his bad side. All this I observed while serving him and his guests.

There came a time when I was considered for a change in position, at this place where we lived and worked. This would have altered my life so completely that I would no longer be living with my master. But I liked living with him and I liked my life, so I was reluctant to take this new position, even though I did not know what it was.

There were men who didn't like the way my master and I were friendly, and they wanted to change that. But my master was so smart, he was way ahead of them. When I first came to him, he observed that I knew things about plants and flowers and herbs that could be used for both cooking and for medicine. Over the years, he built upon my knowledge base with more education about the plants available in Rome. We used the information I had about plants at this place where we worked and lived because there was always fighting happening here. I worked to heal both humans and animals here who were sick or wounded or in any kind of pain.

I became the medicine man in training. I was helpful. This was a very honorable position, and I was the first slave to be called such a thing. This made some people angry, and they wanted to make me go upstairs and train to become a gladiator.

There was no way I wanted to be a gladiator. It was a hard life of training to kill or be killed, nothing else to it. The mean men wanted to change things so much that they tried to kidnap me, but friends of my master made sure that did not happen. They even fought a sword battle about me. The mean men lost and were afraid of my master after that. They never bothered us again.

At this point, the hypnotist shifted his strategy. He said, "Thank you very much. We really appreciate your sharing this life story with us. Now I would like to speak with Kathleen's Higher Self..."

He asked, "Do you recognize anyone in this past life retelling as someone in your present life?"

My clear, confident, immediate reply came from somewhere other than my personal self.

"I have one brother in this lifetime, and my master in the Roman life is my brother in this life. I recognized him as soon as I saw his eyes. The energy in the eyes is the same for both men."

My brother in this life is an emergency physician, a director of hospital emergency departments. In his Roman life, he had a keen awareness of healing practices because he was the director of the training program for slaves who became gladiators for Roman games at the Colosseum.

Past-present-future... they are all here Now.

PeaceKat Star

THE MYSTICAL RAINBOW BRIDGE

or most of my life, I have felt like I've wandered through the veils of existence without direction. I was but a sheep in the cosmic flock, following the shadows of others rather than the whispers of my soul.

One day by a stroke of luck or Divine intervention, I was gifted a free healing session at a local alternative energy healing practice…

A sweet smell of flowery incense and the warm glow of Himalayan salt lamps guides me down the dimly lit hallway. As I navigate the new surroundings, I unknowingly step into a realm that would forever change my life.

Having no experience with alternative medicine, I'm not sure what to expect. As I lay on a massage table waiting for the session to begin, I slip into a calm, relaxed state and get lost in thought as I look up at the ceiling.

After some time, I hear movement and a familiar voice. My new shamanic practitioner friend, Geoff, and the two other energy practitioners I'd met at a spiritual expo a year ago enter the room.

Geoff starts the session by greeting me and asking, "What would you like us to focus on today? You can either share with us what you need or just keep it in your mind while we proceed."

Without hesitation, I respond with frustration in my voice, "I feel I have blocks preventing me from receiving money and love. I constantly work on these areas, but nothing changes. I make progress, but then something happens, and I break down."

I start to cry uncontrollably in front of the three practitioners, who listened empathetically.

Geoff reassures me, "We'll see what we can do today. This is a safe space to share your feelings."

His calm, hypnotic voice helps me slip into a deeper state of relaxation. Closing my eyes but remaining conscious of everything, I feel two practitioners gently placing their arms under my back and begin to sway my body from side to side, like rocking a baby to sleep.

Geoff asks if any of my spirit guides would like to help during the session. To my surprise, I answer automatically, "A robin that I've come to meet has appeared in my head. His name is Steve."

Geoff continues, "Okay, Steve. Nice to meet you! Thank you for coming forward to assist Crystalline. Do you have any messages that can help her on her journey?"

I unconsciously respond in a different voice, channeling Steve. "I can help her learn how to fly like me! And take life more lightly so she can soar!"

My body then unconsciously turns onto my stomach, stretching my arms out to my side like wings. I start inching my body forward like a caterpillar, attempting to move off the table. The practitioners gently guide my body onto the floor.

I hear Geoff's familiar voice fade away, as if I were physically being transported somewhere else, followed by chanting and drumming in the background, but that quickly disappears.

My consciousness then separates from my body. I can tell my physical eyes were closed, but I could see the scene below me.

I am alone in an empty, black space, feeling my body slowly turning over, then flipping faster. I rolled onto what felt like a carpeted floor and then seemingly off the ground entirely, rapidly flying upward into a portal of brilliant, multi-colored lights.

I start to hear a gentle and soothing voice speak in my ear: *Hi, my dear. You are a beautiful soul. You are greatly loved. You have a lot to do here on this planet. I know you have been questioning that for a long time and wondering what your purpose on Earth is.*

I feel myself hovering over the Earth and see a mesmerizing sight: the sparkling blue waters of the oceans and the green and earthy mountain ridges stretched out below me in their natural splendor. I am now looking at the universe through what seems like the lens of an all-seeing God.

Next, a vibrant, extensive rainbow bridge connecting the earth to the rest of space comes into view. As I focus my eyes on the bigger picture in front of me, thousands of glowing light beings ascend from Earth and join me in space, each enveloped by a shimmering, golden bubble of energy.

A majestic voice speaks again to me telepathically: *You are an Earth Ambassador. There are thousands of you, as you can see, ascending from Earth. You all have a great mission to unite the Earth again to the cosmos and all of the other species in the universe.*

Immediately after this godly voice spoke, thousands of different species of beings appear in front of where I was floating. They seem to be the leaders of their kind, all of varying shapes, sizes, and colors. They are waving and bowing as they approach, introducing themselves to me telepathically. I immediately sense that the aura they emit is filled with love, peace, and a profound desire to connect with Earth again and its people.

Although I have never seen creatures exactly like them before in my current life, they all seem familiar to me, as if I have known them from a long time ago in other lifetimes.

This was truly one of the most mystical experiences I have ever had. This powerful, spiritual encounter left me filled with so much love, self-pride, and honor to have this position. The voice I kept hearing telepathically confirmed everything that I was feeling: a sense of accomplishment, freedom, and alignment with my true purpose in life that I had never felt before.

A space of pure white light surrounded me and a beautiful, radiant, and glowing being appeared. Instantly, I knew this being was Mother Gaia herself, in all her splendor, appearing before me. A brilliant, golden light emanated from her, so that I was only able to identify her long, brown, wavy hair, and her white, flowy silk garments that fell so gracefully against her sparkling skin. I was unable to see her face. In the purest of voices—motherly, loving, and gentle—she began to speak.

Crystalline, everything is going to be alright. Follow your intuition. It is time to follow your heart and do what you have always dreamed of doing to help change the world. I chose you to be one of these game-changers because of your soul. You are everything I am looking for, with so much love for people, kind-hearted, compassionate, and pure at heart. This is what is desperately needed in this world. Everything will happen just when it needs to. Trust and allow. You still have so much to do in this lifetime. You are deeply loved.

My entire being filled with overwhelming love, fulfillment, and compassion that I had never felt before.

Just as quickly as I had gone into this out-of-body experience, it felt like my soul and consciousness plummeted back onto the earth plane, back into my physical body.

I took time to move out of a paralysis-type state and started to have feeling back in my arms and legs. I then became aware of my warm and heavy breathing. I realized that I was lying face-down on the floor. My long, black hair was in disarray, and I was shaking and weeping loudly. With my face damp and so many tears streaming down my cheeks, I felt this bright, incredible warmth and overflowing sense of love emanating from my heart. It was beyond any other level of ecstasy I had ever experienced.

I noticed the room was quiet. I was suddenly unsure of where I was or if I was alone. As I regained my composure, I realized I was back in the therapy room. The three practitioners who began this journey with me were peacefully sitting on the ground, cross-legged, in a perfect circle around me.

They let me sit in silence for as long as I needed. When I looked up shyly, my shamanic practitioner friend was smiling at me. "Welcome back. Take your time. How are you feeling?"

I tried to explain what had happened, but it was challenging. No words were worthy enough to express the beauty of that ethereal experience. My friends listened with great intent and patience in their eyes.

I found myself sharing a message with them that I knew, with all of my heart, was from Mother Gaia herself. It was something she wanted me to share with others. With tears of joy filling my eyes, I said, "It all makes sense to me. Everything in the cosmos is the way it is and we are all here for a purpose. Every plant, tree, bug, bird, animal, cloud, and human being on this planet has a purpose. We all matter. There is a plan for everything. We just have to trust and allow."

I believe we are all luminous threads in the grand tapestry of existence. Every breath we take ripples across the universe. There is a sacred plan woven into the fabric of reality. We need only to trust the ancient wisdom that guides us and allows our spirits to dance with the rhythm of the cosmos.

Crystalline Aurora Rose

SONG OF THE ELVES

*S*hortly after I awakened at 15 years old, I found myself doing a project on J.R.R. Tolkien for my high-school Honors English class. After reading *The Hobbit*, and then the full Lord of the Rings series, I was fascinated by how real the world that Tolkien described was. How had he created entire languages, mythos, species, races, and politics at such a grand scale?

A few journeys into reading *The Silmarillion*, I realized he had created entire histories across centuries, even millennia, which backed the stories of his characters and world. His stories told of the origin of the Elves, a people from a "land of eternal sun" who had crossed the great seas to join other races on Middle Earth.

As I spent days in the library finding every book on Tolkien, from his own autobiographical writings to the stories told by those close to him, as well as other avid researchers of his work, I began to discover many things about Tolkien that most of the world still doesn't know.

First, Tolkien was not an author to begin with, but rather a specialized *philologist*, an expert in linguistics across more than seven modern and ancient languages.

He had decided to create a new language, and as he began to form the fine and elegant scripts that would become the Elvish Quenya and Sindarin, he began having dreams and visions of the people who spoke these dialects.

Many of the stories in the Lord of the Rings and his other works emerged as he decrypted the mythology of these languages. In his own words, he wrote what he believed. He was not making up all these stories but rather doing his best to translate them from some other world.

Every layer that I uncovered across his works triggered feelings in me that I could not explain. Some part of me knew I was an elf. Especially as I was awakening, I would find myself in the forests of the ancient Blue Ridge Mountains and feel myself in stillness, hearing the songs inside the land, the rhythms of the wind and trees, and the pathways of the animals across the ridges.

One night, I had a dream. I was walking towards a university building and each step I took got lighter, until I was walking on air, and then flying. I shot upward into the sky and quickly eclipsed the atmosphere, soaring into space above the Earth.

My focus was on the handle of the Big Dipper (Ursa Major), where each of the stars in the handle became triangular membranes. I was suddenly moving faster than logical speeds, passing through each of these energetic membranes, and then through the four stars of the dipper cup…and suddenly I was traveling through a gateway, a wormhole spinning around me for an instant.

I found myself floating towards two beautiful stars, one bright gold and the other a glimmering diamond of white. Between them, I zoomed in on a planet, which seemed to be giving me some details about it in a kind of heads-up display…and the script was elven.

My spirit soared down to the planet's surface, which was very Earth-like but with smaller oceans surrounded by massive purple mountains and massive emerald forests.

I found my way to an open field between these forests with trees as large as skyscrapers and landed on a trail that led down a short hill to a giant, pearlescent white nautilus shell gleaming in the sunshine. Further up the hill to my left was a huge, two-story, round building with a large, glossy black dome arching over the entire top.

I first went down to the shell and discovered it was a home, *my* home, I was certain. Inside, I found an area for food preparation, a writing table, and what seemed to be some kind of stained-glass window on the back side of the entry room. My brain struggled to understand what I was looking at, as it seemed that the colored glass was alive, glowing and shifting as I looked at it. I knew my bed was around the corner in the curve, but I went back outside to keep exploring.

The large, round building on the hill was an observatory, and even though it was bright daylight outside from the primary golden star, inside the chamber, it was dark. All the stars were visible as clearly as though it was a moonless night, and I could also see indicators of ships on the ceiling, traveling between the stars.

The floor was beautiful, tiled in sacred geometry curves like a sunflower and the space had an upper balcony rimming part of the chamber with additional interfaces and tools.

This place was special to me. This place was sacred. Then I woke up.

When I got to high school the next day, I couldn't wait to get to the computer lab and look up "dual sun system." The first hits were articles about a discovery in the Dogon Tribe in Africa.

It turned out that the Dogon had stories about beings from the sky who came down to visit them. The beings created a pool of water, jumped into it, and swam up to the Dogon tribe members. They floated up out of the water and began to teach the Dogon many things.

These beings were called the Nommos and the cave wall illustrations of them by the Dogon make them appear similar to dolphins.

One of the things that the Nommos taught the Dogon was where they came from. On a cave wall in the horn of Africa is a stunning diagram: a perfect illustration of the orbital rotation between Sirius A, and its smaller twin star, Sirius B.

In the article, a story was told about an astronomer studying the rotation of these stars who met an archeologist who was working on the Dogon cave paintings. The astronomer was shocked to see this stellar diagram, which was nearly an exact match to the astronomical diagram they had only constructed based on extremely fine-tuned telescopic studies in the 1980's.

Could these beings, the Nommos, and my dreams, have come from this star system? Then I thought about my studies of the Elves described by Tolkien…a people from a "land of eternal sun…" Perhaps, a dual sun system?

My fascination with elves led me to create a *Dungeons & Dragons* character to play in an ongoing game over the next few years. My character was an elf from a white tower in the elven lands, who had become frustrated with the perfectionism of the elves and left their lands. He wore red robes, signifying his exploration of all kinds of magic and the true knowledge of the universe.

I struggled with his name… I knew it sounded like "Ka-ron," or "Ka'athron," or something similar. I decided to spell his name as "Kharon," pronounced with a deep "ha" sound in the K, and a slightly rolling "r-ron." And suddenly, I knew his full name would be "Kharon Sylvansmoke."

It's worth mentioning that some of the things that happened in that role-playing game were also triggers for my memories, particularly the pending "council of dragons" that was going to happen in the game, but which we never reached. That council of dragons is part of my memories told in *The Dragon Key*.

As the years passed, I could never shake the sense that *I am elven.*

Then in 2005, I had an experience in the middle of the desert of northern Nevada. I was in the deep playa, a prehistoric lakebed where the Burning Man festival takes place.

In the heart of the healing and transformations I went through on that night, I found myself returning to that observatory in the Sirian star system.

My college partner Rastara was suddenly with me in the middle of the desert in her astral body, though her physical body was asleep across the country in Asheville, North Carolina. I was running, and she seemed to merge with my body, and I felt her as though she was inside me. In her dream, she felt like she was running across the desert also, and felt our bodies merge.

We came to a halt in front of an art piece in the middle of endless expanse of desert, with the Burning Man city lights glimmering in spectral flashes far in the distance. The art piece made it look like a fragment of a rainbow was floating above the desert floor, coming out of a prism that was a symbolic, glowing white triangle on a black box sitting on the ground.

My whole consciousness was in a lucid, transcendent state from all the healing I had been through that night. I moved automatically to kneel on the desert ground and place my head into the center of the triangle.

Suddenly I found myself sitting in that observatory, across from Rastara. She was my sister, a gloriously beautiful elven woman. Between us floated a rainbow light field that looked like DNA, in which we were weaving each color harmonic together with our prayer and intention. Each one of the chakras in our bodies were being linked, and we were creating a soul contract.

In this contract, we would lock polarity. She would incarnate as a female, and I as a male, until the contract was complete.

I knew in that moment that we were preparing to leave Sha'Lumea, our elven world with its twin suns and moons, and travel to Terra-Gaia. We would pass through some kind of gates, dropping our current bodies, and travel as souls to this other world, where we would reincarnate. We were linking our soul threads to enable us to find each other after our rebirth, and through finding each other, we would trigger memories of our mission and our past across worlds.

I found myself in deep and full knowledge of this contract that had bound us across lifetimes since we left that world to come to Earth, in the peak of the civilization of Atlantis. A family of elves, migrating to another planet, where they would be with others from many worlds…as one species, and many races.

Together, we knew at that moment, in this crossroads of time—from modern desert to ancient Atlantis to another planet—was the moment to release that contract. So, we stood up together, back on Earth, and we spoke the sacred words of freeing each other. Names came from my lips that were beyond my current understanding, and I freed her by each name, until I finally said, "I free you, Rastara Amarisa."

In that moment, I felt as though a serpent unwound itself from my central core out through my entire spine and I felt a thunderous release of energy. Suddenly, I had waves of downloads pouring into me, visions of being a woman in Atlantis, a priestess in Egypt, and a woman who was my sister again in Avalon… I saw geisha, and dancer, and singer.

Energetic fragments of memory, filled with gifts and lessons she had learned since we formed the soul contract, coursed through me like lightning. I suddenly knew what she had faced, from the deepest fear and pain to the highest joy and bliss.

Many months later, I would discover that she had received a similar download from my soul that night, and all the codes of the masculine incarnations I had since coming to Earth. She had cut her long hair off, which had been down to her pelvis as long as I had known her, and bought a ticket to Ireland immediately.

We each began a journey from there, where we integrated these codes of the opposite sex, the aspects of ourselves shared in the entanglement of souls, and the gifts inherent in those experiences.

Yet for me, this would only be the beginning of my journey through memories across the stars. As I uncovered more about the Sirians and discovered just how many elves had come to Earth, I began to understand, in much greater depth, my soul's grand story.

The journey is deep, the revelations world-shaking. It took 28 years for me to encounter a being who revealed to me my true name from that Sirian lifetime: Kael'Tharan. In that moment, the grace and splendor of excavating our soul are captured. In the tears that streamed down my face, fully hearing my name so clearly and finally understanding so many of the fragments I had gathered across my life, there were crystalline patterns of love that set my cheeks ablaze. I felt a completion, an anchoring, an identity integrated across lifetimes.

And with that identity came relationships, remembering others in this life, who I knew in my lifetimes on other worlds. My love grew through each of them, along with awareness of my self, and my purpose. My life has been sculpted by the architecture of my soul family, as much as I have offered my arts in service to them as well.

As each of the myriad mirrors of myself across all time has converged, I have arisen bearing the crest of my own sacred and sovereign purpose on Earth. I know myself, deeply, truly, fully. And I know what I'm here to do. Now, I offer that gift to you.

Adam Apollo

PART THREE

Experiencing Your Past Lives

The privilege of a lifetime is to become who you truly are.

— CARL JUNG

ACCESSING PAST LIFE MEMORIES

*T*here is a moment when the veil shimmers like a soft breath of starlight, or we hear the sudden thunder of an approaching storm, and we remember. These moments feel more real than a dream, more visceral and lucid than a story. They often carry wells of emotion.

We may not always understand what is happening, but there remains a knowing that comes from within the bones, behind the eyes, deep in the pulse of the soul.

Accessing past life memories is not just about uncovering who you were; it is about remembering who you are and who you have always been.

WHY REMEMBER?

Memories of past lives provide invitations to wholeness along with treasure troves of wisdom and initiations into our fully embodied power.

To recall a past life is to retrieve a soul fragment. Across time, we have left shards of ourselves in the mists, lost pieces of self, waiting to be reintegrated. Whether they take the form of talents long forgotten, the pain of traumas longing to be healed, or a profound sense of purpose that spans across centuries, these memories are not just echoes of lost lives; they are invitations to bring ourselves more fully into the present.

Yet this path must be approached with reverence and care. Not every memory will surface clearly, and many may feel shrouded in the pain and sorrow we have faced before. Sometimes memories come first through metaphor, as our bodies light up while witnessing archetypes in film, reading books, or seeing others who embody aspects of our past self. Other memories are pure sensations rising when we're in proximity to certain people, places, or types of events. Some arrive gently, while others strike us like lightning.

In this chapter, we'll walk the ways of remembrance together while you gain key insights into the practical exploration of your own past lives.

PATHWAYS OF RECALL

There are many methods to access past life memories. What works for one person may not for another, so consider this an adventure where you will try different approaches and learn new skills along the way. Some techniques rely on deep stillness, while others might only be stimulated through more catalytic triggers.

Next are the most commonly experienced approaches to accessing past lifetimes.

MEDITATION ON MEMORY

A quiet mind is the most ancient of mirrors. In deep meditation, we shift from our ordinary thinking into the realm of symbolic awareness, where the soul speaks through images, feelings, and intuitive knowing.

Guided visualizations can help lead the mind down the spiral staircase of time and into memory chambers where fragments of other lives reside. Breathing, grounding, and intention setting are essential here.

Our brains operate similarly to other muscles; when they are used regularly to access certain information, those pathways are strengthened. When parts of our mind and memory are left alone for years, the pathways to access them lose charge and may atrophy.

Regardless of the method you use to access your past life memories, advancing your skills will require practicing meditations where you simply review your memories.

These practices can be done at any time. We are often already doing them with near-term memories of events, people, tasks, and ideas we're working on. However, they are more effective when you're in an alpha or theta brainwave state, so practicing them while you're relaxing in bed before sleep, or after you wake up, is ideal.

Start by looking through recent memories. Put yourself back into various moments and take in your surroundings. Remember the names of those around you if you can. Notice what they wore and reflect on your clothing, feelings, and impressions.

Then move further back, grabbing a memory from months ago and diving into it. Then jump further, to a memory from years ago, and take it in deeply and fully, observing it in as much detail as possible.

Continue leaping further back, in as many or few steps as you desire, back to your earliest memories in childhood. Find one of them that you can feel, where all your senses are alive, and your emotions are present.

This practice provides an initial strengthening pattern for your memory. The more you recall your sensory and emotional perceptions of the past, the clearer your past life memories will be.

You can proceed from this practice directly into one of the past life visualizations below. I recommend starting with my own method, listed next.

NAVIGATING PAST LIFE CONSTELLATIONS

After accessing the memory of a few points going back in your life, travel inside your body and visualize yourself being back in your mother's womb, feeling the warmth and pulse of her heart all around you. Let yourself drift, relaxed, flowing back in time until it gets warmer and brighter. Visualize that you are coming out of the surface of a great sphere of light...your life.

You are connected to this incarnation, fully, deeply, by a thread that can never be broken. And you are free now to explore.

Turn yourself around in your mind and see how the thread of your soul is like a pathway made of light that accesses many different stars shining off into the distance like a constellation.

Now set a clear intention for your exploration, for example:

"I now choose to remember a lifetime that has gifts and relevance to my current life challenges and work."
-or-
"It is commanded that I now access a lifetime where I experienced [person, place, thing] so that I may better understand the connection and purpose of this now."

Watch the constellation of stars; each one is a past lifetime. One of them will become brighter, and you will begin moving towards it. You may pass by other lifetimes, or it might feel as though it is coming towards you. This is essentially an astral space where accessing locations in spacetime does not require linear travel or distance, so any approach that makes it easy for you to imagine this is fine.

For example, some people imagine a large room with many doors. Just make sure that in your visualization, there's always room for more doors! If you see a room, also see the hallways branching to other rooms. If you see a forest with gates, know that you can keep exploring further into the forest to find more gates. I prefer to see stars in the void, as I can also see infinitely (or what seems like it) into the past that way. Let yourself feel the warmth and brightness of the lifetime star in front of you and allow yourself to move into it.

You may see a cascade of colors as the light resolves. You will become vastly more proficient if you learn to clearly visualize yourself entering each of the color rays of the chakras of that body's incarnation from the Crown (white, violet) down through the Third Eye (indigo purple), Throat (luminous blues), Heart (radiant greens), Solar Plexus (golden yellow), Sacral (warm ember orange), to the Root (fire red).

Each layer and color will bring more awareness of yourself in the form you had during that lifetime.

As you come into full presence, first focus on your own body. What are you wearing, and/or what is the shape and form of your body? What do your hands and feet look like? Take in as many details about your own form as you can.

Now explore the environment around you. What is the biosphere like, and what kinds of plants, rocks, weather, and other environmental features surround you? If you're inside a building, what are the structural styles and features? Do you recognize the architectural style or any symbols or elements in the space that relate to cultures you know about in history, or that match things you've had glimpses of, whether by memory, media, or meditation?

Now begin to explore further… If you're inside, what is outside? If you're outside, is there a place you regularly go inside? How did you get to this location? Where did you go after this?

Are there any people around that you know? Is there anyone who is important to you here? If you see them in your mind, you may also ask if you know them in your current lifetime. The answer will likely come more as a feeling than anything, but for some, an immediate knowing will arise, and you will feel your connection with them reverberate through time.

This may require a little time to integrate if the link and memory are strong and new. Breathe with it, allow yourself to feel it completely. There is a reason you're remembering this right now.

Now, are there any sacred objects you have in this lifetime? What are they, and how did you use them? Are they familiar to your current life, or are they ancient or otherworldly? What is your connection to these sacred objects? Focus on one at a time if you see multiple objects. Deeply explore your connection with each.

Depending on how your body feels, and your energy level, you can journey back into earlier points in that lifetime by drifting backward through time and memory, similar to the memory meditation practice. You can also move forward in this life, skimming or diving into different moments.

If you are feeling brave, you can look at the last moments of that life and witness your own death. If you choose this adventure, be sure you also pass through to the other side of your death. There is no need to feel any of the pain or visceral aspects of dying here, though some choose to let themselves have this experience. It is important to let the life go again in this moment and pass through the gates of the death portal. This may feel like you partially move out of the energy sphere of that incarnation, and while hovering outside of it like an angel looking down at your lifetime, you can now inquire about aspects of this lifetime from your life-review state.

"What was the purpose of this life? Why did I experience death in this way? What is the most important lesson from this lifetime?"

As you complete your life-review or finish your explorations, take one or more of the sacred objects you held in that lifetime and keep them with you as you withdraw from that lifetime star. Visualize yourself now floating away from it, turning, and returning to the most brilliant star of them all: your current incarnation.

Merging back into this lifetime, slowly let yourself land back in your body, feeling aspects of your past self as they integrate into your cells, your breath, and all your body parts. Notice how it feels to bring this aspect of yourself fully into the present moment. Let yourself accept all that you have been, no matter how beautiful or difficult those memories may be. We can either choose to accept or reject parts of ourselves, but as long as we reject them, we will continue to face karmic wounds and *sanskaras*, impressions that will cause us to repeat similar mistakes. If we accept ourselves completely, we immediately begin to dissolve any blockages and wounds from the past and begin to receive the gifts we cultivated in that lifetime and others.

When you feel complete, you may want to explore finding a physical object that matches one of the sacred objects from your past life. I have found that this practice has been immensely helpful, as it has enabled me to fully recover skills with certain objects from past lives, such as various sword forms and martial arts weapons forms, calligraphy skills, magical practices, and physical abilities in writing, speaking, dancing, lovemaking, and so much more. As a bonus, I've even been able to integrate new clothing styles that represent aspects of me.

Now let's review a few other approaches to accessing past life memories that you may find useful.

MEMORY GROVE

Visualize a sacred grove with many paths, each representing a lifetime. See each path as a gateway, a door you can pass through to feel yourself enter another one of your bodies, in another time. Let one path call to you or identify one of them through a specific intention. Your intention may simply be exploration.

As you move down the path and cross through the gate, it may feel as though you simply walked through a door and are now someone else.

You can complete many of the above-mentioned practices by noticing what you wear and the shape of your body. What do your hands look like? What smells are in the air? Allow the moments to rise around you and journey through them as deeply as you desire. Sit gently with them, and journal afterward, taking care not to apply judgment to yourself. Focus purely on acceptance and love for yourself.

HYPNOTIC REGRESSION

Regression therapy, when done by trained facilitators, uses light trance states to move through current life memories and into earlier ones. This can be incredibly powerful for accessing visceral, vivid past life events.

Always work with a trusted professional when exploring deep regression. The subconscious can reveal powerful emotional information and vulnerable personal events, and it's essential to feel safe and supported. In addition, you can access collective consciousness archetypes, knowledge of your higher self, and oversoul awareness through hypnosis.

Similar to how a channel operates, our current brains may sometimes limit or filter this information in a way that can lead to inaccuracies. If we don't have enough personal connection or context with the information we are accessing, we may bring through one perspective on that knowledge, but not the full truth of the matter. For example, if you currently have a degree in biology and most of your knowledge is academic, you may have significant distortions if you're translating information about Egyptian magic or advanced technologies and physics from other worlds.

For this reason, while there are often keys that someone can get by accessing the Akasha or collective knowledge during hypnosis, it is my assessment that accessing personal memories from other lifetimes is more useful and accurate.

I have worked with a series of Quantum Healing Hypnosis Technique practitioners and was able to access a tremendous number of details about certain lifetimes. Using this method, I have been able to access some lifetimes that I was not able to reach any other way, most likely because I had not yet built enough mental context to experience them through visualization alone.

After accessing memories through hypnosis, one can then use other practices discussed in this section to intentionally enter those lifetimes and explore them even more fully. Remember that memories accessed through hypnosis will need to be integrated like any other. Acceptance and self-love are critical.

EYE-GAZING WITH A MIRROR OR ANOTHER

When we gaze into our own eyes or another's, without distraction or agenda, something magical happens. The soul begins to rise to the surface and, as the receptor cones in our eyes begin to dilate and slightly fatigue, new layers of light and information may begin to pour in.

In a mirror, your own face may shift, morphing into past forms. When gazing at a partner, faces may cycle through lifetimes, revealing the bonds you've shared. This may feel jarring at first, as suddenly you see an entirely different person in front of you, or you may notice that all of their features disappear into a glowing field while their eyes remain steady and present.

The key to this practice is staying relaxed, calm, and simply observing. You can guide the practice with intention. If you have already had the impression that someone "feels like a Roman soldier" to you, then you can focus your intention on seeing that part of the person while eye gazing with them. Similarly, if you have already had dreams or past life memories come up, you can focus your attention on seeing those aspects of yourself.

Here are some tips and practical steps to ensure you have a successful adventure:

1. Your eyes will shift more quickly if the room is dimly lit, either for looking in a mirror or into another person's eyes.

2. Gaze softly, without blinking (as much as possible). When you blink, your eye cones will reset and things may return to normal, but after a while, your deeper vision will return more swiftly as your eye cones become fatigued.

3. Allow the shifts to happen in your vision and do not react to them. Stay as present as possible and completely still. You may see other genders, ages, or even species.

4. Stay grounded, feeling your body, your breath, and your heart.

SPONTANEOUS RECALL

Many past life memories emerge spontaneously. We may visit a foreign land for the first time and feel as though we've just come home. We might meet someone, and a part of us knows them instantly, feeling deep comfort and trust...or strong caution and wariness. We smell a scent and are flooded with emotion, possibly combined with visual, audible, or other sensory flashes. These are golden threads, the subtle, sacred breadcrumbs of the soul.

While we can't force these spontaneous states of recall to happen, we can create conditions that we are more sensitive to and experience them more often.

When we move through life with a deeper sense of listening, finding the stillness inside of us and quieting the mind, everything we experience becomes more vivid. As we practice cultivating our energy field (biofield, *chi, qi,* vital force, prana) through Tai Chi, Qi Gong, Reiki, Tantra, or internal martial arts, we become more sensitive to the dynamics of the connections between ourselves and others, as well as our bonds with places and things. We start to become aware of exactly how entangled we are and in what proportions our quantum fields are linked. When we dig deeper, using the structured inquiries discussed in this book, we can discover exactly why we have these connections.

For some people, these spontaneous recalls start happening around intense spiritual experiences and awakenings. As we increase our awareness and expand our consciousness, we naturally begin to notice much more about ourselves, our lives, and our connections across time.

If you're having these experiences, honor them. Write them down in a journal to contemplate later. Sit with them and let them unfold themselves. Each of these experiences is like a pin on a map, and as you open to those memories more, you will place more pins and expand the territory of your awareness of other lives.

THE EMOTIONAL LANDSCAPE

When past life experiences arise, they often come with emotional surges—grief, love, fear, rage, ecstasy. Memory is not neutral; it is built from frequency and vibrational states. This is energy that is in motion, yet sometimes frozen in a snapshot of our past. As we become aware of that moment, the energy moves again, and we experience *emotion.*

Emotion is evidence that the vibrational state of the past is surfacing into our present experience. The emotions are how you know it's real.

Yet care is always needed. A traumatic death, betrayal, or loss in a past life can trigger intense feelings in the present, and if we block or resist these feelings, we stifle the energy that wants to move through us. We might put up a wall that keeps us from remembering and accessing these parts of ourselves.

In her book *Light Emerging,* former NASA astrophysicist Barbara Ann Brennan proposes that all illness is simply stuck energy. Her work has shown that simply by identifying our restrictions and contractions around certain ideas and feelings and releasing them through intention and various energetic healing practices, even cancers and seemingly incurable diseases vanish from the body. She defines symptoms as the body's alert systems, notifications telling us that we need to open a part of our body, energy, and mind in more specific areas, allowing the energy to flow.

Have you ever known something to be true at a deep level but struggled with sharing it or speaking it aloud? You might have faced challenges in the throat around that time. Have you had a hard time digesting different events happening in your life? You may have noticed digestive issues around that time.

Our bodies are energetic systems. As we allow that energy to flow, our immune systems, nervous systems, and all other systems can reach their peak states of health.

When we access past lives, we're bridging old energetic experiences into the present. It is essential to allow, accept, and let the energy currents of those past experiences flow through us. Regardless of how intense or hard the memories may be, the wave of feelings will pass. The more you embrace them and love yourself through these awakenings, the faster those feelings will move through the fires of passion and into the gentle fields of elation and inspiration.

Always practice grounding and self-care. If needed, seek support from a guide or therapist trained in spiritual integration. After a powerful memory, take the time to integrate. Eat food that is grounding. Touch the Earth. Journal. Breathe slowly. Give the body time to digest what the soul has revealed.

SOUL HEALING AND LIBERATION

There are sacred moments in the remembrance of past lives when wounds arise, not merely to be seen, but to be healed. For some, this begins as a subtle ache in the chest, the sudden arising of an unexplainable fear, or a deep well of grief that feels too large for this lifetime. For others, it may erupt through the nervous system like lightning, a trauma long buried that suddenly finds a voice.

This chapter is for those moments, for the echoes that demand release. For the soul fragments longing to come home. For the freedom that comes only when we no longer define ourselves by the pain we carry, but by the light we've retrieved through healing.

HEALING UNRESOLVED TRAUMA FROM OTHER LIFETIMES

Trauma from other lifetimes can leave imprints in our soul across various layers of our energy body, and as I theorize, down into our DNA. These imprints can surface as recurring emotional patterns, somatic tension, or repeating relational dynamics that make little sense in the context of this life. You may have done "all the work" on a certain issue, and yet it lingers.

This is often a sign that the origin is deeper, older, *transdimensional,* and *transchronological.*

Past-life trauma may be encoded in the body as cellular memory. It may reside in the astral layers of your energy field. It may show up in dreams, spontaneous memories, phobias, or even birthmarks. It is essential to understand that it can, and will, inevitably be healed. The simple question is: when would you like to complete that part of this soul lesson you have chosen? This type of soul healing liberates not only your current self but influences all future potential timelines from here and affects your perceptions of the past, integrating echoes of various astral timelines simultaneously into a single, sacred thread.

Yet there is a bigger question that every soul must face, unfolding it layer by layer as we come to understand what trauma truly is and why we have chosen it as part of the Divine dance.

Are you ready to accept full responsibility for your own journey, end your victimization, and restore your Divine sovereignty and power of eternal choice?

Even if you're not ready for that leap, you can begin your journey with the consideration of what that might be like. What would it mean to regain command and access memory, skill, and magic from all the aspects of yourself across time? To begin healing trauma from another lifetime:

1. Acknowledge the memory. As soon as it arises, take a moment to stop whatever you are doing and focus on it. Find a safe and quiet space where you can drop in and begin to work with the memory. If it arises during a group practice or experience, if possible, request others who are present to hold space for your experience.

2. Allow the memory to fully surface. Let it rise with all the pain, emotion, and layers of experience. Welcome all of it without resistance, acknowledging that it is a memory of something that

happened in the past and is not currently happening, even though you are accessing it now. Speak aloud what you remember or feel, even if it makes no sense yet.

3. Feel it in your body. Notice where it lives. Does it cause tension in your shoulders? A collapse in your solar plexus? A clutching of your heart? Let breath return there and spend some time simply breathing into different areas of your body, focusing your attention and energy to bring presence into those places.

4. Give it a voice. Let your past self speak, expressing the experience and what happened. Let yourself feel and remember any moments after that experience, either still incarnated or after death. Feel the moment and allow it to pass all the way through in your consciousness. Let the river flow.

5. Offer presence. Now bring your breath and awareness back into the present moment. Bridging between now and the trauma in the past, become the guide and guardian for your past self. Recognize that you have learned many other lessons since then. Hold your past self in your awareness. Say aloud: "You are safe now. I am here. I will not abandon you."

6. Reprogram the past choice. You can leverage several Theta Healing techniques to change your relational energy to this past self and begin to integrate it more fully. For example,

   "I forgive myself for this past experience. I forgive those who caused me pain in this past lifetime."

   "I clear and remove, cancel, and resolve all magic, curses, or spells cast on me that fail to serve my highest and best good related to that lifetime."

   "I clear and remove, cancel, and resolve all contracts from that lifetime that fail to serve my highest and best good."

"I clear any and all resentment, regret, and rejection I feel from that lifetime."

"I accept and receive the Divine perspective on this past life experience."

7. Journal and integrate. Meditate on that version of you and deepen your contemplation. Work with other past life access practices to remember more of the events prior to the trauma and get to know your life better. What were you feeling at various times? What happened in the flow of events? What does this part of you need you to know and integrate now, to complete this lesson?

These acts of conscious witnessing allow frozen fragments of the past to thaw. Your nervous system begins to rewrite the story. They do not change events through denial but integrate the full truth of the events and their sacred purpose through resolution and intention.

RELEASING KARMIC ENTANGLEMENTS WITH OTHERS

Karma is often misunderstood as cosmic punishment. In truth, it is more like a magnetic field of unresolved energy created by action, intention, and relationship. When we carry unresolved karma with another being, it can feel like an invisible thread tugging on our choices, emotions, and circumstances, lifetime after lifetime. Karmic entanglements can manifest as:

- Persistent emotional attachment or resistance to someone
- A cycle of repeated conflict, betrayal, or abandonment
- A deep, inexplicable sense of familiarity or obligation
- Difficulty cutting ties, even when the relationship is painful

The key to dissolving karmic bonds is not avoidance or disconnection, but transformation through awareness, love, and choice. To release a karmic tie:

1. Identify the bond. Who continues to occupy mental and emotional space in your life, even beyond reason?
2. Feel into the original agreement. Sit in meditation and ask, "When did this begin?" Let images or emotions arise. Often the origin point is a vow, a debt, a betrayal, or a death.
3. Revoke old contracts. Say aloud or write:
    "I now revoke all vows, contracts, and entanglements that no longer serve my soul's evolution. I release you. I forgive you. I free you—and I free myself."
4. Replace the energetic imprint. Visualize yourself and the other person in a golden field of light. Imagine handing back any energy that belongs to them, especially any cords or energy threads you notice, and calling your own energy home. You can also ask for that energy to be purified and neutralized by Divine Source. Thank the person you had the ties with and then let them go.

Some karmic bonds are rooted in deep love and don't require cutting, but clarification. These relationships may evolve into new expressions, free of old burdens. In this way healing karma doesn't sever connection, it purifies it.

Consider families and their various bonds. At certain ages during a child's growth into adolescence and adulthood, the structure of the existing agreements and energetic bindings between them and other family members becomes outdated. These are critical moments when the child needs to clear these energetic attachments and find clarity in their own self-perception and sovereignty as an individual. From here, they can rebuild energetic bonds with their family, creating new agreements or energetic relationships.

Sometimes, this also means that adolescents or adults end their bonds with close family, simply because they are no longer willing to be compatible with the patterns imposed on them by family members. This could be temporary or more permanent, depending on what the needs are.

In this same way, by healing karmic bonds with others, you're resetting the field between your souls and gaining an opportunity to redefine it or end the bond entirely.

RECLAIMING GIFTS AND SOUL FRAGMENTS

When trauma occurs in this life or another, parts of the soul can fragment and hide. This is a form of spiritual self-protection. In shamanic traditions, this is known as *soul loss*. A piece of the soul may retreat at the moment of violence, betrayal, or grief. Yet with love, we can call those pieces back.

Often, soul fragments hold gifts we need in our current life: confidence, creativity, sensuality, vision, strength. As you heal, these gifts begin to return, rising like buried treasure from within. Here is a simple process to reclaim lost soul parts:

1. Set sacred space. Create a container with candlelight, breathwork, or a short grounding meditation.
2. Name the gift. Ask yourself: "What aspect of me feels missing?" You may feel a longing to reclaim your voice, your power, your innocence, your magic.
3. Call it back. Say:
   "I now call back the part of me that carries the gift of [name the quality]. You are welcome here. You are safe. I receive you with love."
4. Feel the integration. You may experience tingling, warmth, tears, or even a memory returning. Let the sensation flow through your body.

5. Anchor it. Take an action that embodies the returned part. Sing. Dance. Speak truth. Create. Touch the Earth. Let it live in you again.

Sometimes, soul fragments are tied to specific ages or events. You might retrieve your seven-year-old self who once felt abandoned, or your past life priestess self who lost her temple. Whatever form it takes, welcome her, him, them, home.

Each time you call a piece of yourself back, your field becomes more radiant, your gifts more embodied, and your presence more magnetic.

THE ROLE OF FORGIVENESS AND LOVE IN TRANSCHRONOLOGICAL HEALING

There comes a point in soul recovery where effort alone cannot cross the threshold. Where technique is not enough. Where remembrance and reprogramming give way to something greater.

That something is: *Love.*

Forgiveness is not about condoning harm. It is not a passive acceptance of injustice, nor a dismissal of what was lost. Forgiveness is a radical act of liberation that cuts the cords that bind you to pain. It is the reclaiming of your energy from the entanglement, not for the other, but for yourself.

When we forgive, we acknowledge the wound, feel it fully, and then consciously choose to release the energetic hold it has on us. In doing so, we dissolve the karmic charge at the root. This is *transchronological* healing: an act in the present that echoes through time, unwinding the consequences of lifetimes.

Forgiveness is also a *transdimensional* frequency that carries memory into harmony across all our different bodies, from the physical to the Akashic and beyond. Love—true, unconditional love—is the force that transmutes density into light.

What does this mean? Imagine threads of various colors of light, but when they get tangled into balls in certain ways, light is hidden inside the ball, and in this case the brightness strangely dims. Yet as you begin to send the feeling of love to this ball, the threads that form it shift from tangles to precise geometries, and suddenly all the threads and the light inside every layer become visible and amplify each other.

In music, we experience harmony and beauty when there is space between the notes. During music production, the mastering process for tracks and albums is an art involving separating each of the different frequency octaves inside the music, allowing each instrument or tone to have its own individual space in the waves of sound.

Based on the research of the HeartMath Institute and the work of Dan Winter, a modern physics philosopher, as well as others, we know that our physical heart emits an electromagnetic field, and this field begins to take on a specific geometry when we experience love. According to Dan Winter, this is a Golden Mean Ratio waveform, a perfect spiral of compression and expansion that can cross between all the octaves, from the smallest waves to the largest waves.

In my unified physics models, love provides the key geometry for spacetime to curve (gravity); for matter to form (protons); and for information to enter and exit each proton so that everything can communicate with everything else. This geometry is illustrated through the pentagon, pentagram, five-pointed star, and pentacle simplex. It is the origin of the Golden Mean Ratio.

From a metaphysical standpoint, this would mean that when we experience love, we simply create a fractally recursive wave field that matches the natural communications and memory structure of spacetime itself. So, at a soul level, we're simply realigning our past perception to the actual truth of the beautiful, geometric masterwork of grace.

In the soul's journey across lifetimes, we often become entangled and experience these bundles of distortion not from failure, but because we loved another so deeply that we betrayed ourselves or were hurt by those we loved most. Betrayals and losses cut the deepest when love is present, as one is strongly influencing the field in love states, and an act of deep inner collapse has the strongest effect from this state. And so, it is also through love that we heal, unwinding the collapsed and distorted bundles of energy we've knotted in the past back into the light lattice of truth hidden within those moments. To practice this kind of healing, try the following:

1. Recall a specific painful memory, or connection with an individual, where you have felt this deep inner collapse. Let yourself feel all the unresolved emotions: grief, rage, sorrow, longing. Do not suppress or rush this step. It is essential to allow yourself to feel through all the layers of the threads that became the knot. Let your heart be cracked open by your persistent arrow of awareness seeking the center of it all, the love in it.

2. Visualize yourself and another, if appropriate, in a space of sacred light. This may look like a temple, a garden, or a neutral realm of light or void. If this involves another person, let the other soul appear before you in a form that feels symbolic and safe.

3. Speak your truth. Tell yourself (or them) what you remember. What you felt. What it cost you. Let the energy move through your voice or your inner awareness.

4. Then say, when you are ready:
    "I release you. I forgive you. I love you. I free you, and I free myself."

5. Let the light embrace you (and them). See the layers of energy in you aligning back into perfect harmony, breathing with love into your body and theirs. If this is with another, see your bond between you transmuted—not severed, unless you choose it—but returned to harmony, no longer carrying the weight of the pain.

Sometimes, you may need to repeat this ritual more than once, especially if the karmic loop is deeply entrenched. That is okay. Forgiveness is a spiral, not a switch.

And sometimes, the one you must forgive is yourself. For the choices you made, and for the ones you didn't. For the ways you abandoned yourself in moments of fear or confusion. These acts of self-forgiveness are among the most powerful you can offer, for they heal not only this life, but all others where you doubted your worth, betrayed your soul, or dimmed your light.

As you learn to forgive, you clear the inner mirror. Love begins to flow again. And with it comes clarity, peace, joy, and presence. You no longer carry the burden of the past. You begin to carry only its wisdom.

ANCHORING YOUR LIBERATED SELF IN THIS LIFE

Healing is not the end of the journey; it is simply a rebirth of the Self and the beginning of living a truly liberated life.

After retrieving memories, clearing karma, and calling back soul fragments, you find yourself entering a threshold of deeper embodiment. You face the sacred task of anchoring all that you have reclaimed into the present moment, into your daily life, your choices, your voice, your expression, and your body.

This is the integration phase, and it is where healing becomes transformation, and you may experience *transfiguration*. To anchor your liberated self:

- Create sacred rhythm. Practice a morning ritual that acknowledges your wholeness. It may be as simple as placing your hand over your heart and saying, "I welcome all that I am, across time and space." This anchors your timeline sovereignty.

- Embody your gifts. If you reclaimed a voice from another life, speak. If you retrieved an artist, create. If you found a priestess or warrior, let those archetypes shape your posture, clothing, and expression. Let the energies live in you.

- Choose aligned relationships. As you rise into your full self, certain dynamics may no longer fit. Release what constricts you. Call in those who mirror your sovereignty and honor your soul.

- Stay in communion with your soul. Keep tracking your inner world. Journal. Meditate. Listen to your dreams. Let your newly retrieved self, speak and guide you. Allow your intuition to evolve as your multidimensional and transchronological awareness grows.

- Serve from your healing. Let your journey become a light for others. You do not need to teach or preach, just embody who you truly are. Your presence alone, your beingness, will become a tuning fork for others to remember who they are.

This work will change the way you experience your entire life. After all, you are a living constellation, with pieces gathered from across the stars. These segments will begin humming together in harmony as you integrate your past. Your field will begin to sing with the frequencies of many lifetimes, unified in the now.

This is the art of soul sovereignty. Not seeking to achieve perfection, or even completion, but rather simply being an embodiment of all that you are, now.

You are free to choose, again and again, from your deepest truth.

You are whole.

And from here…the real adventure begins.

THE DIVINE WISDOM
OF THE SOUL

s our journey of remembering lifetimes continues, we may begin to experience moments when all the separate lives we've lived begin to shimmer as facets of a single, radiant jewel. We experience our core star, our most essential central operating system of the soul, blooming like a supernova. The faces, names, languages, lifeways, all the aspects of ourselves begin to spiral inward like petals folding into the center of a blooming rose. This is the ultimate integration. A soul that once looked outward across lifetimes begins to turn inward toward the eternal.

Past life recall is often approached through the lens of identity: *Who was I? What did I do? What wounds remain?*

Yet in time, we begin to see that each lifetime was less about building an individual ego and more about adding depth, texture, wisdom, and resonance to a singular, magnificent song.

This chapter is a hymn to that symphony. It is an invitation to view your soul not as a scattered series of disconnected stories, but as a spiral of Divine purpose unfolding through form. It is a journey into the multidimensional mandala of self—a self that spans like a web across the stars, yet finds its center in your breath, right here, right now.

THE SPIRAL PATH OF SOUL EVOLUTION

From the causal plane, the level of existence where many chronological patterns, lessons, relationship dynamics, and archetypes reside, we can trace the unfolding of a soul as it incarnates again and again to learn, love, and liberate. Each incarnation is a new stanza in a great poem. Some are sharp and short like haiku. Others are long epics full of trial and triumph. Yet all are essential.

As we deepen in awareness, we come to understand: We are not a single story. We are the *author.*

Spiritual evolution is not linear; it spirals. Through lives of royalty and servitude, conquest and contemplation, passion and penance, the soul is shaped. Every loss sharpens compassion. Every betrayal polishes discernment. Every death becomes an invitation to love more deeply in the next life.

This, then, is the true miracle of remembrance: not only that we can look back, but that we can bring forth the gifts earned in all those lives and let them bloom again in this one.

THREADS IN THE GREAT PATTERN

Imagine, if you will, the universe as a vast spherical loom, an ancient and eternal architecture weaving the threads of every soul into a living tapestry. Each planet woven in threads like a ball of yarn extending across solar systems, interconnecting planets and forming a galactic web. Yet the threads of souls also extend across galaxies, forming networks of light and energy that mirror the structures of neurons and tissues within our bodies.

This is the macrocosmic view of our journey. We are not alone. We are strands in a masterpiece beyond imagination, and every one of us is essential to its beauty.

Aspects of this image, a great loom weaving souls as threads, was powerfully explored by author Robert Jordan in *The Wheel of Time*, a series whose metaphysical roots run deep. In his universe, all souls are threads in the *Pattern*, woven by the great Loom of the Wheel. The Wheel spins out lives, not at random, but as part of a grand, elegant, intelligent choreography of existence. No thread exists in isolation, each touches thousands of others, influencing the whole design.

Jordan also introduced the concept of *Ta'veren*: souls so radiant, so aligned with Divine purpose, that the Pattern itself bends around them. These souls reshape destiny through the strength of their presence. Their love, courage, or sacrifice becomes a gravitational center, drawing others into alignment and altering the weaves of the world. And so, the tapestry of time is patterned around the choices of these souls.

Is this merely fiction? Or is it a reflection of something your soul already knows?

In truth, we all have moments where we become *Ta'veren*—times when our actions ripple outward through time, calling others home to their hearts. When our devotion changes the lives of those around us, and when our light is so bright, it begins to bend probability.

This is an obvious pattern in great leaders, as many people flock to follow their patterns and experience their lives, even from a distance. When we let the full power of our many lives bloom within us, the archetypal songs that emanate from us bring forth others who resonate with us and want to join our symphony.

From a metaphysical perspective, the pattern is fractal. Each thread, each soul, is not a straight line, but a spiral of memory and intention, a colorful strand woven with choice and transformation. Some weave loosely, dancing in and out of other threads. Others bind tightly in karmic braids, repeating lessons until the knots are undone.

And then there are those rare souls who begin to see the weave. Who remembers not only their own past lives but the sacred interconnectedness of *all* lives. Who remembers how to see the songlines of the Earth, the magnetic meridians of Gaia's dreaming, and the geometry of soul groups, councils, and celestial families.

You may be one of these. If these words stir something ancient within you… then you are already awakening to your place in the loom.

Your soul is not a single thread. It is a braid of colors, textures, and archetypes, interlacing across time like a multidimensional strand of spiritual DNA. Some filaments gleam with starlight from lives in distant systems. Others hum with the heartbeat of ancient Earth lineages. Together, they form your living ray of Source, expressed in fractal brilliance.

So ask yourself:

What threads am I weaving now?

What threads do I wish to strengthen?

What colors, what gifts, what echoes of past lifetimes want to return and sing through me now?

The Great Loom is alive, and the pattern is not fixed. It is ever-changing, always responding to your choice, your awareness, and most importantly, your love.

LIVING WITH PAST LIFE AWARENESS

Once we begin to recognize the vastness of our soul across lifetimes, we realize something astonishing: this wisdom, this power, is not meant to remain in the clouds. It is meant to be *embodied*. Lived. Breathed. Danced.

The mystic does not awaken to the stars only to escape the Earth; they awaken to *infuse* the Earth with starlight.

Living with past life awareness is not about clinging to past identities. Rather, it is the art of allowing gifts within our memory to emerge through our presence. It's knowing you were once a healer and trusting your hands now to move with full awareness of that healer within you. It's feeling the fire of a warrior rise in your belly and knowing when to stand firm, create space, and develop the art of fighting without fighting. It's sensing the voice of your temple singer and letting her sing through your modern tongue or in languages of light from other worlds.

Each identity, each facet, is a note in your inner orchestra. With practice, you learn when to call upon each note intuitively, dancing through your own form and rhythm.

In ancient Egypt, there are stories of the D'jedi, a group of magi who were said to have constructed the pyramids; almost nothing else is known about them, and the actual mechanisms for the construction of the pyramids remain a mystery. George Lucas popularized these mysterious magi as the Jedi Order, perhaps with more truth than he realized, capturing the true Galactic Lineage behind the seemingly impossible stonework and technologies of the ancients. Yet the D'jedi are not lost, as they awaken in anyone who seeks to know the true wisdom of their soul across lifetimes.

The D'jedi who practices the art of soul memory learns to feel into the moment and allow the right self to arise, not with ego, but with intuition. Not by trying, but by attuning, such that the emergent aspect of self is more authentic to that moment than remaining in your modern world identity.

APPROACHES TO CULTIVATING THIS DANCE OF IDENTITY

Sense the Field. Learn to feel the energy of a situation before reacting. Is this moment calling for a mystic? A protector? A lover? A sovereign leader? Understanding the archetypes of your different lifetimes gives you an easier access point to the energetics of specific skill sets across lives.

Quiet the Ego. Let go of the need to *be* someone. Instead, become the clear vessel through which the soul's many aspects may speak. This is not about conceptual projection, but deep, present embodiment. Let your body become the body of your other lifetime identity. You are now them, they are now you, and there is no difference, so your mind doesn't need to make any meaning or egoic construct out of it.

Move with Memory. Sometimes you'll walk into a place and remember the stones. Or you might meet someone and feel recognition beyond words. Honor these moments, they are *activations*. Let life awaken you to the keys, through synchronicities. Let memory arise naturally and develop your ability to contemplate, to explore presence within those memories, and to practice embodying them further as part of your daily life flow. If you're ever feeling stuck or feeling a lack of growth in this area, simply travel somewhere new, somewhere you feel a past connection with.

Just as we shift tones depending on the person we're speaking with, we shift energetic facets depending on what our soul is being asked to do and where we do it. We become a kind of living ceremonial toolkit, where our lifetimes play like instruments, and our presence acts as an invocation for grace and magic.

GIFTS WE CAN UNCOVER

Accelerated Skills: Languages, music, martial arts, calligraphy, writing, singing, dance, chess, weapons skills, healing modalities, business development, sailing, horseback riding, and much more.

Innate Wisdom: Cosmic awareness, galactic remembrance, elemental alchemy, ancient magic, ceremonial traditions, archetypal systems, finance, legal frameworks, etc.

Sacred Technologies: Leyline mapping, crystal programming, sound healing, and various forms of sacred planetary magic that may originate in Atlantean, Lemurian, and interstellar lineages.

Even more subtle are the ways this awareness begins to shape our emotional body. We develop deeper compassion because we've been both a villain and a hero. We understand forgiveness because we've carried both the wound and the blade. We develop wisdom because we've seen the spirals long enough to recognize when a pattern is ready to break.

And in daily life?

You may suddenly know how to comfort a crying child or sense when to pause before making a deal. You may dream of a temple and find it on a map the next day. You might feel ancient grief while walking through ruins or experience a wave of joy while dancing under the stars. As you familiarize yourself with many different lifetimes and identities, you may even surprise yourself when one emerges at the perfect moment and you reveal a hidden skill or ability you did not know you still had.

This is what it means to live with *transchronological* awareness: to dance through the now with the full library of your soul behind your eyes.

We are not here to escape our bodies or past lives. We are here to inhabit them fully, so that through us, the entire spiral of existence may become conscious.

ETHICAL SOVEREIGNTY IN SOUL WORK

With great remembrance comes great responsibility.

As you begin to reclaim lifetimes of wisdom, skill, and power, it is essential to walk this path with integrity, discernment, and love. Past life awareness is not a tool for dominance or validation. It is not about spiritual superiority or proving who you once were. It is a sacred key, meant to unlock more compassion, not more ego.

The deeper truth is this: we are all ancient. Every soul has walked worlds, worn crowns, held suffering, and touched the stars. What matters most is how we carry that awareness now.

If we attempt to use our past life identities to make others see us differently, this is an act of hiding, in which we are putting forth a projection of our ego. However, when we simply embody the truth of who we are and are unconcerned whether someone perceives us as our current self or past self, the soul speaks for itself.

When we look at the world and see how many people try to make others believe they are this or that famous person by their aggrandized self-important declarations, we see that the real detriment is often narcissism or a messiah complex. Someone may become extremely upset or volatile with others if they are not fully accepting or acknowledging that self-projection. And often, others don't feel comfortable accepting it, because it's not true, it's simply an archetypal projection.

When someone has played a massive role as a famous person in other times, they have often had to navigate the difficulties of fame and the complexities of collective projection. While it is possible they may still be caught in ego patterns from these lives, it is also possible that they walk the world more quietly in this lifetime or take extreme care in how they share such truths about their past. This is self-honoring and sacred work, and it may be work you need to do as well.

These are deep spiritual mechanics. Hiding behind the mask of a false ego can deepen sanskaras and reinforce karmas, but liberating the ego through presence with the truth and self-awareness can unwind old patterns and energetic blocks, clear karmas, and empower us.

KEY APPROACHES TO ETHICAL SPIRITUAL LIBERATION

Honor the Journey of Others. Not everyone is ready, or willing, to remember, and that is perfectly okay. We cannot force remembrance, nor should we try, as each soul unfolds in its own rhythm. You may recognize a past life connection with someone who does not feel it. That's not a failure of yours, or theirs. It's an invitation to love them as they are now, without condition or agenda. The greatest gift you can give is presence without pressure.

Discern Personal Truth from Collective Archetype. It is easy to feel resonance with famous figures or mythic stories. And sometimes, these are true memories. But many souls carry archetypal echoes—overlapping roles within the same collective pattern. You may not have been *the* Cleopatra, but a priestess in her lineage. Not *the* Merlin, but one of the many who carried that frequency or title. Let go of needing certainty. Let the resonance guide your healing and gifts, not inflate your persona.

Use Power to Liberate, Not Control. With soul memory comes access to influence: magnetic presence, intuitive knowing, and even subtle energetic manipulation. Be mindful. Always ask: "Is this in service to their sovereignty? Or to my desire?" True spiritual mastery uplifts. It never coerces. Let your presence invite, never ensnare.

Stay Grounded in the Now. Past life memory is seductive. It can become a way to escape the discomforts of this life. But your soul chose this moment, this body, this incarnation. The lessons of the past are meant to empower your purpose now, not replace it. Anchor into the present and use your memory to enrich this life's service.

Tend to Your Healing First. Before offering soul work to others, ensure your own field is clear. Remembering a lifetime where you held power does not mean you are ready to wield it again. The past carries wounds as well as gifts. Tend to the trauma. Integrate the lesson. Then the power will emerge clean.

When we walk the path of remembrance with humility and reverence, we become catalysts beyond our own evolution, for the awakening of humanity. Our very presence begins to emanate the codes of transformation.

This is how the future is changed: not by preaching the past, but by embodying the eternal now.

BECOMING THE AVATAR: LIVING THE ALL-TIME SELF

When you have walked the path of soul remembrance, healed your ancient wounds, integrated your archetypal gifts, and anchored them into your present life… you arrive at a threshold.

Not an ending.

A becoming.

You begin to live not as a fragment of your soul, but as the full fractal of it. You walk the world as a living avatar with a holographic embodiment of your soul's complete lineage shining in every cell.

You become a vessel through which the wisdom of your entire causal continuum flows freely. The healer, the mystic, the scientist, the warrior, the priestess, the rebel, the king, the child, the star-being… all coalesce in a single breath. *Your* breath.

This is the *All-Time Self*—not just an awakened human, but an integrated Soul-Being expressing across the dimensions.

This doesn't mean perfection. It means presence. It means the ability to draw on vast reservoirs of knowing, without attachment. To respond to life with depth, not reaction. To be a tuning fork for grace because you've attuned your field to the frequencies of remembrance and love.

Your mind becomes crystalline in clarity. Your emotions become oceans that no longer drown you, but through which you swim like a Dragon of Light. Your body becomes a temple of many gods, now walking as one.

To embody the All-Time Self is to let your choices be guided by soul truth, not fear; to walk the Earth not as someone seeking to arrive, but as one who is the arrival. The prayer. The answer. The presence.

And as you live this way, you unlock something extraordinary.

Your field becomes medicine for the world.

You don't need to speak, your being teaches.

You don't need to explain, your presence heals.

You don't need to lead, your resonance guides.

In the holographic field of unity, every fully integrated soul becomes a beacon, a lighthouse for others to remember their song. We awaken as a network of avatars singing across the nodes of time.

And this, dear adventurer, is how the New Earth is born—not from one messiah, but from the flowering of millions of remembering souls, walking awake, walking whole, walking in full presence, now.

So, take this final breath with me, here at the edge of the spiral:

You are not merely healing. You are becoming.

You are not just remembering. You are re-membering—reweaving— yourself into the whole.

You are not waiting for your moment. *You are the moment.*

Now rise.

Embody.

And let the Universe witness the return of your radiant soul in all its timeless glory.

INVOCATION OF THE
ALL-TIME SELF

I call forth the Soul of me
that spans across stars and centuries,
the Breath that remembers
and the Flame that endures.

I summon the Healer, the Lover, the Warrior,
the Scholar, the Priestess, the Child of Light—
all faces of the One I Am,
braided in the loom of eternity.

I stand now as the Living Thread,
not torn from the Tapestry,
but woven with luminous intent
into the Great Pattern.

I offer my past not as burden,
but as brilliance.
I release all bindings
to who I thought I was

so I may become
who I have always been.

I vow to use my memory for Mercy,
my gifts for Grace,
my power for Peace.

Let the stars remember me.
Let the Earth sing through me.
Let the Now open as a gate
through which I walk whole,
radiant,
and free.

I am the All-Time Self.
And I am here.

THE GENTLE SPIRAL HOME

*T*his book began as a map through the Akasha and has unfolded into a mirror for the soul.

Across these pages, we've explored what it means to remember and awaken to the timeless presence of past lives not as curiosities, but as living layers of who we are. We've walked the roads of science, soul, and stardust. We've spoken of trauma and transcendence, gifts and grief, soul families and cosmic journeys. We've faced the past not to get lost in it, but to reclaim the light we left there, and bring it home.

Through my own journey, I have come to understand that past life remembrance is not a destination. It's not about arriving at a singular identity or proving a theory. It is a sacred ongoing act of love and self-discovery, a continual unfolding of who we truly are beneath the masks of time. There are so many layers to us, to who we truly are, that simply revealing the essence of our own eternity is a spectacular adventure.

There were countless times when I couldn't have walked this road alone, without the blessing of beloveds across time, from soul friends and teachers to sacred mirrors and lovers. Many people have helped me along the way. With their support, I've recovered lost fragments of myself, rewoven my sacred threads of purpose, and illuminated key memories I thought I'd never find. Some came for a moment. Some came to stay. But all my beloveds brought purpose.

The practices in this book are invitations, flowing streams, each one leading you deeper into your own truth. They ask you to trust your intuition rather than follow rigid steps, to honor your timing rather than require some Saturnian discipline, and to let memory be a gift, not a burden.

As you continue to explore your Akashic field, remember that each life is a teacher. Every incarnation adds its own color, its own tone, to the great masterpiece of your being. You do not need to have all the answers now. Let your soul unfold gently, like a flower in the morning light. Let remembrance arise not through force, but through presence.

And always, always return to humility.

For the soul is vast, but it is also tender. Memory can exalt or ensnare, depending on how we hold it. Walk this path with reverence. Let each step be a prayer. Let each new discovery remind you that there is so much more to learn, and that this mystery is a blessing, not a flaw.

You are not alone in this. You never have been.

So, I leave you here, not at an end, but at the beginning of your next spiral, where new lifetimes may bloom in dreams. Where your present becomes more alive through the past, and where grace, that silent companion, walks beside you in every step.

Remember gently. Love deeply. Live now.

The Akasha is open.

And your story… continues.

MEET OUR SACRED STORYTELLERS

NAN AKASHA is an Ancient Mysteries Teacher, Jaguar Medicine Woman, and priestess initiated in Egyptian, Greek, and Mayan Mystery Schools. Founder of the Return of the Priestess Sacred Magic Mystery School, she guides sacred retreats, courses, and soul journeys focused on past life healing, spiritual awakening, and multidimensional remembrance. nanakasha.com

MONICA ALONSO leads a women's moon circle and is the guardian of an etheric crystalline temple in Mexico. She provides sessions with crystals, light codes, light language, and Arcturian-Pleiadian Reiki.

ELYN AVIVA, PHD, MDIV., is a writer, spiritual explorer, and reluctant medium. She writes about sacred sites, quests, and pilgrimages. She and her husband live in Girona, Spain.

CRYSTAL BELLA AMBROSE has experienced life through an unfiltered connection to the unseen. These lifelong multidimensional experiences led her to a path of bridging physical and spiritual realms. Through decades of guiding others and her own soul-led travels, she continues to help empaths awaken their gifts and reclaim their light. Author of *Soul Hangry*. velvetmoonrising.com

ANNETTE ASSMY is a dream teacher, shamanic practitioner, priestess, and founder of the Mystery School of the Soul. Initiated as a Pampamesayok, she is called Earthkeeper.

HEATHER BRUCE-BENING is a constant journal writer and embraces the many entries of meaningful events that help shape her life-past present and future. She believes life is joy hidden beneath the folds of life experience.

MIRIAM "MARYA" CORNELI, teacher, energy worker, Seimei practitioner, spiritual medium, and consciousness researcher, holds that past life recall shines a light into the miraculous kaleidoscope of collective soul energy we are all part of. By studying those lifetimes, we can increase compassion and the evolution of consciousness.

CHERI EVJEN is a wife, mother, and grandmother who splits her time with family in Wisconsin and Nevada. After completing a corporate career, she has a mission to build a community and provide resources to support other grandparents of child loss. thegrievinggrandma.org

LESLIE GRIFFITH has been on the healer's path in this lifetime; working as a nurse for 43 years in large academic hospitals, receiving a Masters Degree in Counseling Psychology with Health Emphasis, and is now studying Spiritual Mediumship. She honors all on the path of remembering their Divine Nature.

ANN MARIE HOLMES is the author of *Earth Spirit Living*, an educator, Feng Shui consultant, and Nature stories writer.

DEBBIE IRVINE, M. COUN., (Australia), is a counselor, dreamwork and shamanic practitioner. Midlife she experienced life-threatening illnesses, Primary Immunodeficiency Disease, and permanent disability. Guided by dreams and spiritual insights, Debbie experienced profound transformation during her studies and travels overseas, encountering deep mystical experiences that changed her life and healed her. debbieirvine.com

NICHOLAS JOYCE works with small social and ecological groups to nurture connection and clarity. He listens deeply, observes what's emerging, and helps design simple, practical systems to fit the flow of the group.

JOANNA OPENCHOWSKA KAZMIROWICZ is a Polish born Australian. She is an ex clinical nurse and recall healing practitioner who has developed her own method of human energy scanning to help clients.

LAURA MAHER is a published author of the true-life novel *Auntie Mom* and her debut children's book, *I Love to Be Me*. She makes her home in California, where she continues to write stories that inspire and uplift.

MARK MCADAMS' mission is to be of service in assisting others on their spiritual journey. He employs alternative healing modalities: QHHT© past life regression, Somatic Mindful Guided Imagery©, shamanic ritual, and he is a Level III Reiki Master. These modalities contribute to holistic growth on multiple levels. back2balancesolutions.com

PAUL J. MILLS, Professor and Director, University of California San Diego, is the author of the 2023 Gold Nautilus Award winning book, *Science, Being, & Becoming: The Spiritual Lives of Scientists.*

SUSAN MELNIKOW is an Elder Transformational Midwife and a Minister of Walking Prayer. She spent forty years birthing babies as a Nurse Midwife and now provides mentoring for all of life's transitions. She values living in sync with Spirit and loves facilitating connections to personal Divine pathways. transformation-tree.com

IDA RA NALBANDIAN is an author dedicated to exploring the power of language to inspire and cultivate expansion of the greater good, and more compassionate world. Her book *Jacob's Magic Vegetables: How Loving Kindness Grows* was an Amazon bestseller & Dreamvisions 7 Radio and TV Network Children's Book of the Month.

PAMELA D. NANCE, MA in Cultural Anthropology is certified in past life regression, hypnotherapy, healing touch, shamanism, spiritual dowsing and is an investigator into the survival of consciousness after death for four decades.

BARBARA ROSS GREANEY is an ordained minister with the Universal Brotherhood who explores spirituality in her writings, meditations, healing work, soul path readings and channeling. She lives in Leesburg, FL.

CRYSTALLINE AURORA ROSE is an author and transformational and spiritual life coach who has been helping others find their calling in life to live more passionately and full of love.

SIMONE SENISIN, PHD is a retired educator living in Australia on Gulidjan Country. Eternally grateful for the experience of soul's expression in this human life — the connections and community. She writes extensively about spirituality, on matters of healing grief through grace, gratitude, love and laughter. simonesenisin.substack.com

PEACEKAT STAR is fascinated with all that shows us how to remove limitations from our perceptions. She assists others in how to do the same through the services she offers.

HELLEVI E. WOODMAN is an entertainer, author, dancer, and yogi. A multidimensional dreamer and explorer of Earth's magical mysteries, she shares practical tools for conscious living, dreaming, and dying.

MEET THE AUTHOR

Adam Apollo is an international speaker, educator, and founder whose work bridges the frontiers of science, spirituality, and systemic transformation. He has offered insights on global transitions, unified physics, technology, and human evolution at the White House, United Nations, and major conferences and festivals around the world.

His exploration of past lives began with vivid spontaneous recall in his teens and evolved into three decades of transpersonal research and soul-level integration. He supports others in unlocking their soul memory to reclaim purpose and power.

He is the cofounder of UNIFY, which reaches over 10 million people monthly, and leads two education and technology companies: Access Granted and Superluminal Systems. He is a core faculty member and architect of global academies including the Resonance Academy for Unified

Physics, the Guardian Alliance Academy for self-mastery, and the Visionary Arts Academy, serving over 150,000 students worldwide.

Adam is the author of *The Dragon Key* and many online courses on subjects ranging from sacred geometry and quantum physics to astral travel, high magic, and multidimensional embodiment. He has been featured on Gaia TV, Coast to Coast AM, and numerous documentary films.

A martial artist, DJ, and poet, Adam Apollo also worked with indigenous elders during Prayer Runs for World Peace and experienced direct extraterrestrial contact in 2005. He is currently building CoreNexus™, a decentralized operating system for planetary regeneration, fusing economic innovation with social impact.

Adam's work catalyzes remembrance—awakening soul, science, and civilization into harmonic alignment.

Learn more at https://adamapollo.com